THE PLOT AGAINST
SOCIAL SECURITY

THE PLOT

AGAINST

SOCIAL

SECURITY

*How the Bush Administration
Is Endangering Our Financial Future*

MICHAEL HILTZIK

HarperCollins*Publishers*

HarperCollins books may be purchased for educational, business, or sales promotional use. For information, please write: Special Markets Department, HarperCollins Publishers, 10 East 53rd Street, New York, NY 10022.

FIRST EDITION

Printed on acid-free paper

Library of Congress Cataloging-in-Publication Data is available upon request.

ISBN 0-06-083465-X

05 06 07 08 09 ❖/RRD   10 9 8 7 6 5 4 3 2 1

To Deborah, Andrew, and David

Contents

CONTENTS

Preface

S HORTLY AFTER the 2004 presidential election, with a surge
of bombast and hokum forming around the proposed privatization of Social Security, I decided to focus one of my twice-
weekly columns in the *Los Angeles Times* on the issue. The
fundamental question I asked was how a movement to transform the United States' most effective social insurance program
into a system of individual investment accounts could have sur-
vived the scandals and financial losses associated with the most
recent stock market crash. I also asked whether Social Security's
principles of shared risk and communal assistance weren't worth
preserving, and suggested that the privatization lobby's por-
trayal of the program as fiscally unsound was nothing but fear-
mongering.

The piece evoked a prodigious response from readers.
Among the cascade of emails, letters, and phone calls I received
were many that expressed appreciation for my effort to correct a
tide of misinformation, some that ridiculed my short-sighted
complacency about a supposedly bankrupt system, and still

others that charged me with the crime of "liberalism," whatever that is.

By far the greatest number exhibited unfamiliarity with or confusion about the basic facts of the Social Security program—how it is paid for, what governs its financial condition, and whether it can be sustained. They posed questions like these: Isn't the trillion-dollar trust fund merely a fiction? Doesn't the system owe $10 trillion it can't repay? How can it continue when two workers support every retiree? Why should I pay taxes for a program that won't exist when it's my turn to collect?

Plainly, decades of propaganda aimed at undermining Social Security had fulfilled their purpose by spreading fear, uncertainty, and doubt about the program's principles and future. That was disturbing enough. Then, toward the end of the year, the Bush administration launched a campaign that I came to think of as a domestic version of Operation Shock and Awe, an onslaught of such bunk and balderdash about Social Security that the news media and the program's professional defenders were hard-pressed to keep up.

The White House's brief against Social Security exemplifies an epigram generally attributed to Mark Twain: a lie can travel halfway around the world while the truth is still putting its boots on. It's packed with numbers that sound meaningful but are hollow and deceptive. It's based on claims asserted as truth although they have long since been proven false or, at best, remain subject to debate. Its presentation is carefully designed to conceal the ulterior motives, ideological and financial, of its promoters.

Anyone who has taken the time to examine the facts knows, at the minimum, that Social Security is not facing "bankruptcy"—not now, not in the near future, not at any time in the next 75 years even under pessimistic economic forecasts. It is not $10 trillion in the red under any reasonable definition of debt and liability. The decline in the ratio of workers to beneficiaries from 16:1 to 2:1—an especially favorite statistic in the right-wing bill of indictment against Social Security—is almost useless as a measure of the system's health: the sharpest decline, from 16 workers per beneficiary to 5, took place during its first 20 years of the program's operation, when the number of covered retirees soared from zero to 14 million without shaking its foundations. The subsequent, more moderate, decline from 5:1 to 3:1 has taken 45 years, more than twice as long. The rate is slowing and may soon reverse.

But most people don't have the time to subject this torrent of misstatements to a truth test. That's not surprising. Most people are too involved in the daily struggle to earn a living, raise their children, and fend off what President Franklin D. Roosevelt called "the hazards and vicissitudes of life" to consider why President George W. Bush wishes to dismantle the one government program designed to insulate them from those very burdens.

As the campaign against Social Security has gathered steam, the misstatements of fact have become wreathed in the kind of self-contradictory rhetoric that passes in America today for political discourse. In promoting a manifestly partisan and ideological program to alter the system, President Bush promises "not to play politics" with the system. Insisting that the system needs to be modernized to reflect the demographic and economic realities of the twenty-first century, he proposes a return to the naked individualism of the 1920s. He says all options for reform have always been on the table, although he required the blue-ribbon appointees to his own reform commission in 2001 to pledge that their proposals would include the creation of private investment accounts and wouldn't involve any increase in the payroll tax.

In its current incarnation, as in all the guises it has donned over the last 70 years, the plot against Social Security aims to propagate, and then exploit, public ignorance about the program. This book is an attempt to redress the balance of information.

The literature of Social Security reform is copious, complex, and abstruse, as befits a 70-year-old program that covers more than 154 million contributors and 47 million recipients. Many individuals have helped me find a way through the jungle of statistical studies, administrative reports, philosophical and ideological tracts, and legislative proposals that has grown and flourished over the decades. Among those who gave their time to talk or correspond with me on numerous aspects about this issue are Robert M. Ball, Alicia H. Munnell, David Langer, Olivia S. Mitchell, and Michael Tanner. Many others contributed to my understanding via insightful writings that are acknowledged in the text wherever pertinent.

My agent, Sandra Dijkstra, urged me to undertake this project, inspired me with her enthusiasm, and provided peerless advice and assistance in shaping the result. My editor at Harper-Collins, Tim Duggan, guided the manuscript with an effective and elegant touch that enabled it to take form quickly. At the *Los Angeles Times,* my editors, especially Business Editor Rick Wartzman, responded generously to my need for the time to undertake this work.

My wife, Deborah, provided her characteristically sharp journalist's eye for crucial turns in the ongoing debate, issues that cried out for treatment in this book, and material that would enrich the final product. Finally, my two sons, Andrew and David, members of the cohorts due to retire in 2083 and 2086, inspired me to do my part to ensure that Social Security, for all its imperfections and uncertainties, will still exist to serve them decades from now, as it has served millions of Americans for decades in the past.

THE PLOT AGAINST
SOCIAL SECURITY

Chapter One

The Bush Blitz

ON JANUARY 11, 2005, President George W. Bush perched himself on a stool onstage at the Andrew W. Mellon Auditorium in Washington, flanked by a few dozen ostensibly ordinary American citizens.

Addressing his audience from beneath the gilded colonnade of the grand old government hall, he thanked them for coming that day "to talk about one of the great causes of our generation, and that is how to strengthen and save Social Security for generations to come." Gripping a plump microphone and speaking in his characteristic tone of folksy earnestness before a national television audience, he reiterated his already familiar admonition that the national pension and disability program was mortally ill. His onstage companions, including a young Utah dairy farmer, an ambulance company operator from the state of Washington, a Maryland businesswoman and her elderly mother, and a bright young official from the Social Security Administration itself, listened raptly as he warned that Social Security might well not exist when the time came for them to retire.

"If you're twenty years old, in your mid-twenties, and you're beginning to work, I want you to think about a Social Security system that will be flat *bust . . . bankrupt,* unless the United States Congress has got the willingness to act now," he said. "And that's what we're here to talk about, a system that will be bankrupt."

The best way to protect themselves from that dreadful outcome, he said, was to keep some of the money they were paying each year into this rickety Depression-era system and invest it by themselves, for themselves. And he was determined to push a law through Congress setting up a system of private retirement accounts that would enable them to do exactly that.

George Bush had been thinking about Social Security reform at least as far back as his tenure as governor of Texas, when he had invited experts to his ranch to chat about the program's future. He made reform a major plank in his 2000 presidential campaign, and became convinced that his endorsement of private accounts had been an essential factor in his electoral victory. Once inaugurated, he promptly made good on his campaign rhetoric by appointing a blue-ribbon reform commission to craft a privatization plan. But as a domestic policy initiative Social Security got overwhelmed by the 9/11 attack and, subsequently, by the Iraq war.

Immediately following his reelection, however, the president launched a blitzkrieg on Social Security. In nationally televised speeches, appearances before blue-ribbon White House economic conferences and interviews with trusted journalists, Bush, renowned for his ability to stay "on message," delivered the gospel of radical reform, often repeating the same phrases by rote. The centerpiece of this program was a system that would allow workers to withhold a few percentage points of the 12.4 percent payroll tax from the system and invest the money on their own. The reform would relieve Social Security of its crushing deficit, he contended, while giving every American a personal retirement stake that could be bequeathed to survivors. "At the same time that you manage your own account, you own your own account," the president proclaimed to the Mellon Auditorium crowd. "I *love* promoting ownership in America."

Administration officials and Republican legislators fanned out to the Sunday TV talk shows to warn of the imminent crisis and pitch privatization as the solution. Callers to the Social Security Administration's help line heard not music while they languished on hold, but messages warning of the program's looming insolvency and the necessity of hasty, dramatic change. White House fundraisers started to squeeze their most dependable contributors to pay for a television campaign budgeted at a cool $100 million. The campaign's architects billed the effort to remake Social Security as "one of the most important conservative undertakings of modern times" and "one of the most significant conservative governing achievements ever."

Their goal was no less than to dismantle one of the last surviving edifices of the New Deal.

President Bush has called his proposed policy "a promise to reform and preserve Social Security."

In fact, his proposal would neither reform nor preserve Social Security. In the name of preservation, it would destroy the nation's most comprehensive social insurance program and replace it with a system bearing enormous costs and risks for millions of workers and retirees.

The Social Security privatizers dress up their proposal with the premise that all Americans will be able to earn annual investment returns in the stock market of 7 or 8 percent a year, *after* inflation—a figure that makes the putative return on Social Security payroll taxes look paltry indeed. The market will make every American owning a private account a millionaire upon retirement, they say. (The *New York Times* headlined a recent op-ed piece on the topic by former treasury secretary Paul O'Neill, a devout privateer, "Who Wants to Be a Millionaire?")

What they don't tell you is that many economists question the likelihood of consistently earning such a return from stocks. In fact, they say it's almost impossible. For U.S. equities to turn in that kind of performance over the next several decades, the overall U.S. economy would have to grow at a pace that, all by itself, would place Social Security on the strongest fiscal footing in its history—not only far from bankrupt, but rich enough to bail out the rest of the federal government. (This is according to the Social Security system's own estimates.)

The privatizers don't mention, moreover, that the new system would require such complicated administrative oversight that the Social Security Administration, perhaps the most efficient arm of the federal government, would have to hire as many as 100,000 new employees. (This estimate comes from an executive at Fidelity Investments, which *favors* private accounts.) Account management fees—which would flow to some of the same financial services companies backing the privatization campaign—would eat up a good portion of the workers' savings.

All this for a reform that even the White House acknowledges would do nothing to improve the Social Security program's long-term financial condition. On the contrary, the transition to private accounts would deprive the program of trillions of dollars that would otherwise finance benefits already promised to millions of American workers and their families. To make up the loss, the system might have to slash benefits by 30 percent or more—the only such benefit cut in the program's 70-year history, and one that might produce a new generation of impoverished elders. That's the part of the so-called reform that the White House hasn't been so eager to publicize. The privateers are all but saying that to save the program, they must first destroy it.

What the privatization of Social Security would do is shift more financial risk onto ordinary citizens. This would continue a recent trend that has made daily life more unpredictable for millions of workers at all levels of the wage scale. Downsizings and outsourcings, automation and globalization have all made the concept of secure lifetime employment a thing of the past. Gone is the confidence that one's yearly earnings will follow a safe upward trajectory throughout one's career, vanished along with the promise of affordable health care and a secure corporate pension.

President Bush's response to the increased risk borne by Americans in the workplace is to subject them to even more risk. In implementing the "ownership society" of which he speaks so glowingly, he intends to erode the social programs that for decades have helped people meet the cost of medical care, job training, disability, and retirement—at the very moment when employers are cutting back on the same benefits.

As Jacob Hacker, a Yale University political scientist, recently observed, "business and government used to see it as their duty to provide safety nets against the worst economic threats we face. But more and more, they're yanking them away."

Such a policy bears dangers not only for individuals, but for society at large. "If we get the ownership society wrong," warns the economist Robert J. Schiller, "growing inequality and social unrest are likely to follow."

Since its enactment in 1935, Social Security has faced numerous threats and prevailed over them all. It was opposed at birth by conservatives who considered it a costly and unjustified government intrusion into private lives; in the postwar years by Republicans determined to write an epitaph to the New Deal; and in the 1980s by Reagan revolutionaries who launched their campaign to shrink the federal government by attempting to demolish its largest entitlement program.

But the system has never faced a threat as dangerous as the one it faces today. The leader of this assault has at his disposal voting majorities in both houses of Congress, as well as a claque of tame ideologues, economists, columnists, and television commentators. George W. Bush and his rightist acolytes command a megaphone with which they intend to dominate public debate over the program.

The January 11 event at Mellon Auditorium opened a new phase in this campaign. The president aimed to show that average Americans from all walks of life shared his concern about the future of Social Security, and that they hungered for the right to own and control at least a small part of their investment in retirement.

Throughout the 45-minute session, he stuck doggedly to his talking points, at turns joshing with his stagemates as though they were all stars on a TV talk show and chilling them with auguries of the financial shadows hanging over their future.

He told Josh Wright, 27, the Utah dairyman, that Social Security would be "flat broke" by the time Wright reached retirement age. With Bob McFadden, an African-American pharmaceutical executive, he commiserated about the system's inherent unfairness to black citizens, "who die sooner than other males do." He prompted Andrew Biggs, 37, an associate administrator of Social Security, to agree with his assessment that "we have a *problem.*"

He talked about how "most younger people in America think they'll never see a dime." He said the system was a looming $10-trillion drain on the economy ("That's trillion with a 'T'—that's a lot of money, even for this town."), a Ponzi scheme ripping off the American worker. He called it hopelessly outdated, created for a distant time when "most women did not work outside the house and the average life expectancy was about 60 years old." In the old days, he observed, 16 workers paid in to the system for every one retiree taking money out; now the ratio was closer to 3 to 1 and would presently shrink further. He shook his head mournfully. Confidence in the system's survival was at a low ebb. The chief obstacle to placing the system on a firm financial footing was "politics." But "those days of politicizing Social Security, I hope, are in the past," he reassured his audience.

He came armed with a new idea: the creation of personal savings accounts filled with "safe," secure, highly profitable investments. These would grow over time, fueled by the magic of compound interest and the marvel of stock market appreciation, at a rate that handsomely outstripped the return on Social Security taxes. An "interesting idea—it's certainly not *my* idea, because others have talked about it," he said. Because, after all, he reminded everyone, Social Security taxes are *your* money.

As it happens, most of President Bush's factual assertions were false.

For all that he repeated the term "bankrupt" to describe the future of Social Security (five times in the space of his 45-minute appearance), the term is inappropriate. According to the system's official estimates, under current law it will still receive enough money every year to cover most of its obligations to beneficiaries even after 2041, when it will be entirely dependent on payroll taxes to fund benefits. Although President Bush warned Wright that the system would be "flat broke" by the time he reached retirement age, the fact is that in 2045, when Wright could retire with full benefits at age 67, Social Security would be taking in enough money to pay 74 percent, and possibly 100 percent, of his entitlement—without a single change in tax rates or the benefit formula.

The president overstated the size of the system's deficit and misrepresented the significance of the worker-retiree ratio, which is largely irrelevant to Social Security's future financial condition. He made mathematical blunders, rewrote the program's history, and treated its projections for the next 75 years—actuarial prognostications based on a dizzying number of very rough estimates—as though they were as immutable as the laws of physics.

The January 11 event possessed another feature characteristic of Bush administration news events: it was rigorously stage-managed. Although the participants onstage were described as ordinary folks, they were ringers.

Sonya Stone, the Washington-area businesswoman who eloquently described for Bush her fears for the future and her desperation to see the system "improved with the establishment of personal accounts," described herself as "a divorced mom raising three children." She didn't mention that she had been an executive of the Heritage Foundation, a conservative Washington think tank that is one of the architects of the privatization campaign.

Scott Ballard, the owner of an ambulance service who fretted that he lacked any control over how his Social Security taxes are spent even though "it's my money that I'm putting into the system," is the son of one of the most prominent Republican politicians in Washington state. His trip to the president's show was all-expenses-paid, courtesy of FreedomWorks, an anti-tax and pro-privatization lobbying front headed by former Republican congressmen Jack Kemp and Dick Armey.

Josh Wright described how his crusty dad had set him down in the barn one day and warned him, "Don't depend on Social Security," as though this were a nugget of folk wisdom. He didn't add that his father was not just another dairyman. State Senator Bill Wright, long a member of the Utah legislature's conservative Republican "cowboy caucus," had battled for years for low taxes and reduced government interference in family life. He once created a statewide furor by asserting that no faithful Mormon could "in good conscience support the official tenets and substantiated agenda of the Democratic Party." Josh Wright is also a member of FreedomWorks.

As for Andrew Biggs of the Social Security Administration, whom Bush introduced as an "expert" on the looming crisis, he has spent years on the staff of the Cato Institute, the libertarian think tank that has provided the intellectual ammunition for the attack on Social Security for a quarter of a century.

The nation's leading newspapers and broadcasters failed to report much of this background, or to draw a connection between the phoniness of the lineup of ordinary folks and the phoniness of the president's pitch on Social Security. For all anyone knew, these people had ended up onstage with the president of the United States, feeding him straight lines about the insolvency and injustice of Social Security, because they had won some sort of random cosmic lottery. Nor did the press expend much effort questioning the president's math or historical analysis, other than to quote Democratic "critics" as having a different viewpoint, as though the future of Social Security were merely another partisan Beltway flap.

But the current debate about Social Security is more than a battle between equally valid interpretations of the real world. The privatization campaign may utilize the language of hard economics—of deficits, long-term liabilities, and tax burdens calculated as a share of gross domestic product—but at heart it is ideological and partisan. As a hyperenthusiastic White House aide wrote in January 2005 in an internal memo that promptly found its way into print, the Social Security battle is one that "can help transform the political and philosophical landscape of the country." The aide saw the issue of Social Security's future as a weapon against the Democratic Party. "Increasingly the Democratic Party is the party of obstruction and opposition," he wrote. "It is the Party of the Past."

Indeed, this is a battle over the values America should stand for—over whether the nation upholds the tradition that a community takes care of its most vulnerable members, or returns to the era of "rugged individualism," where the strong and the lucky prevail and the unfortunate fall by the wayside.

One of the remarkable aspects of the modern attack on Social Security is how closely it resembles the political and ideological attacks of earlier decades. Today's plot is part of a continuum dating back to the congressional debate over the program's enactment. At that time, as the Brookings Institution economist Henry J. Aaron observes, the program was opposed by "a vocal minority of Republicans entirely unreconciled to the idea that government should play a role in providing income for retirees."

Their views resurfaced in the platform of Kansas governor Alf Landon's 1936 presidential campaign against Franklin D. Roosevelt. They keep returning, decade after decade.

Waging this battle on the fog-shrouded battlefield of economic theory often provokes the general public to tune out. That's because although economic statistics have the flavor of empirical facts, they're almost always frustratingly obscure. Not for nothing is economics labeled "the dismal science."

The haziness has allowed misinformation, misinterpretation, and outright deceit to infect reform campaigns throughout Social Security's history. As one progressive public policy expert predicted when the Clinton administration took up the issue of Social Security finances, "It is a good bet that we soon shall be surrounded by a swirl of half-truths and outright howlers about how to 'fix' the nation's premier social program." His words could have applied in 1935. They certainly apply today.

Those who comprise Social Security's clientele and constituency—96 percent of all American workers pay into the system and stand to collect an old-age or disability stipend—deserve to understand where ideology ends and hard facts begin. This book is an effort to establish the dividing line.

What gives Social Security its unique stature as a government program is that it is not a simple pension plan but a hybrid composed of a conventional defined-benefit program, a system of disability insurance, and a social safety net.

By far the largest group of its beneficiaries are retirees and their families, who account for 33 million of the 48 million persons who cashed Social Security checks in 2004. Largely through the system's old-age program, nine out of ten elderly Americans receive benefits averaging $11,460 a year for single persons and about $18,900 for couples. The program provides more than half the monthly income of two-thirds of these recipients; for one in five it's the sole source. Without this money, the number of Americans over 65 living in poverty would be about 36 percent higher. (Among those 80 and older, the figure is 45 percent.)

It should be plain that this is a boon not only for the recipients themselves, but for their families, who might otherwise be required to provide for their aged parents at a time in their lives when they may also be trying to raise their own children and save for their own retirements.

Other benefits serve smaller but nonetheless significant groups. Disability payments are made to another 8 million Americans, including 1.7 million children. Another 6.8 million recipients are deceased workers' survivors, mostly children, whose benefits average $10,700 a year.

It's not surprising, as the economic analyst Jeff Madrick observes, that many of these secondary insurance benefits are "easily forgotten or have come to be taken for granted." For their recipients, however, perhaps much more than for the old-age beneficiaries with whom the system is most usually identified, Social Security is often all that stands between them and destitution. Privatization advocates often overlook the impact of their proposals on these beneficiaries, who would be almost impossible to serve through a system of private accounts.

Social Security has another feature that would be very difficult and costly to replicate in a private system: its benefits are inflation-indexed and last as long as the recipients live. The value of a stipend that can't be outlived or eroded by higher prices is incalculable for any given beneficiary, because it's impossible to know how long any retiree will live beyond age 65, or what potential mischief inflation might do to his or her resources over time. Between 1970 and 1980, for example, two oil-price shocks and other economic factors slashed the purchasing power of the dollar by more than half. For people living on fixed incomes, the process of figuring out how long a retirement nest egg might last became a painful and panicky rite of old age, alleviated only by the rising value of the monthly Social Security check. In recent years, inflation has stayed quiescent. But given the implacable nature of the economic cycle, it is sure to flare up someday.

As a safety net, Social Security redistributes wealth, transferring resources from richer to poorer within any given age cohort. (In Social Security parlance, a cohort is any group of workers or retirees born in the same year.) To see how this operates, let's consider three workers, all born on the same day in 1939 and retiring in 2004 at 65.

Fred, whose wages were at or above the maximum on which the payroll tax is assessed every year of his working life, will receive an initial monthly benefit equal to about 38 percent of his average monthly earnings. (This is known as the "replacement rate.") For Joe, who earned a median wage, the replacement rate will be about 54.5 percent. For Bill, who was at the bottom of the pay scale, earning the minimum wage every year, the rate will be 73 percent.

Implicit in these figures is the notion that lower-paid workers have a lesser chance of accumulating the nest egg needed for a comfortable retirement outside of Social Security, and therefore need a larger stipend relative to their career wages to secure the necessities of life. The best-paid, by contrast, theoretically have had a better opportunity to build private resources that they can use to support their accustomed lifestyle after retirement.

Anti-tax ideologues resent this aspect of Social Security. They complain that it unfairly assesses the haves to pay for the upkeep of the have-nots. But it's worth noting that while Social Security old-age benefits are generally progressive—meaning in this case that they are relatively more valuable for poorer workers than the affluent—other aspects of the system are regressive. The annual income subject to the payroll tax is capped (at $90,000 in 2005). Any wages earned in excess of the ceiling, therefore, thus lower a taxpayer's overall rate. For example, a worker earning $90,000 in 2005 will pay 6.2 percent of his or her income, or the maximum of $5,580, to Social Security. (The worker's employer pays a matching $5,580.) For a worker earning $180,000, however, the same $5,580 tax amounts to a tax rate of only 3.1 percent. By contrast, most middle-class and low-wage workers pay more in payroll tax than income tax.

Affluent workers also tend to collect benefits for a longer period after retirement because they live longer, on average, than their lower-paid counterparts—indeed, low-wage workers are statistically less likely to live to retirement age and collect any benefits at all. (The gap in life expectancy between high earners and low earners, moreover, is widening fast.)

Social Security's critics have burrowed deep into these figures in attempting to prove that the system is a bad or unfair financial deal for one or another segment of society—for young as opposed to old, blacks rather than whites, two-earner rather than single-income couples. At a fundamental level these exercises miss the point of Social Security. The program was not designed to maximize the financial return on every worker's payroll tax, nor to provide all the necessary resources for every worker's comfortable retirement. Rather, it was designed to provide basic protection from the bad luck, bad decisions, and bad times that can befall almost anybody.

That makes the financing of Social Security a complex art,

because defined benefit plans are by nature highly sensitive to economic changes. Many times over the years, Congress has been forced to adjust the payroll tax, the retirement age, the benefit formula, the size of the cost-of-living increase, and other technical aspects. Lawmakers have not always gotten the fixes right—which isn't surprising, because economic conditions are always changing, and always unpredictably. Sometimes reforms designed to set the system on a secure footing for decades have proven inadequate within a few short years; a huge miscalculation about inflation and wage growth in the 1970s, for example, awarded retirees a wildly more generous cost-of-living increase than was warranted, bringing the system near collapse in the early 1980s.

But none of those changes provoked the doom-and-gloom rhetoric, the predictions of obsolescence, or the kind of attack on the fundamental principles of the program seen today.

One reason Social Security has been immune from such a challenge until now is that even its most severe critics have had to acknowledge that in fulfilling its basic goals it has been the most successful government program in American history. Even President Bush, while outlining plans to dismantle it, called the program "an incredible achievement, if you think about a piece of legislation being relevant for nearly 70 years."

Social Security is the government's largest single program in revenue as well as outflow, accounting for nearly 22 percent of all federal spending. But while the federal budget operates at an overall deficit, Social Security does not. Its 2005 surplus—the difference between what it spends on benefits and administration and what it collects in taxes and interest—is expected to be about $178.6 billion. The program lends this surplus to the federal government by purchasing interest-bearing Treasury securities, which it will eventually have to redeem for cash to cover retirement benefits for the baby-boom generation.

Despite its size and complexity, the Social Security Administration has been remarkably efficient. The program's annual administrative fees run less than 1 percent of benefit payments; the cost of a private annuity account offering the same combination of lifetime benefits and inflation protection might be higher by a factor of 12 to 20.

Even more striking, the system has been entirely free of financial scandal. The last 70 years have witnessed two major stock market crashes; fraud convictions of legions of corporate chief executives and financial whiz kids; the destruction of one presidential administration by criminal activity (and the near-destruction of another); dozens of senators, congressmen, and executive aides charged with wrongdoing; and the squandering of the defense budget on $640 toilet seats and other extravagances.

In all that time, Social Security has never been sullied by fiscal scandal. Although it has been the target of a determined and well-financed group of ideologues for decades, the program has never opened the door even a crack to the charge that it is wasteful or imprudent with the taxpayers' money.

Who then would profit from a so-called reform plan that does not save Social Security, but blows it to smithereens? Not wage earners, retirees, and the disabled. They would lose the program's lifetime pensions, its provision for annual cost-of-living adjustments that protect monthly stipends from inflation, and its guaranteed coverage for spouses and children.

The investment and insurance industries, however, would stand to gain an unprecedented amount of revenue. According to an economic study by University of Chicago economist Austan

Goolsbee, the baseline Bush administration privatization proposal to divert one-third of the payroll tax to individual accounts could produce management fees for Wall Street totaling more than $1.1 trillion in today's dollars over the next 75 years—"by far the largest windfall for financial managers in American financial history."

No wonder that when a pair of conservative strategists mapped out a program in 1983 to undermine the public image of Social Security and to promote private investment accounts as an alternative, they identified their natural allies as "the banks, insurance companies, and other institutions that will gain from providing such plans to the public."

Through the years, the political techniques of Social Security's *faux* reformers have remained remarkably consistent. They can be divided into three general categories: (1) Undermine public confidence in the system's future. (2) Question its relevancy to the contemporary workforce. (3) Bemoan its effect on worker behavior and the overall economy.

Undermine public confidence

When he signed the act creating an unprecedented social insurance program in 1935, Franklin D. Roosevelt understood that public opinion would be the system's stoutest bulwark against its enemies. Indeed, one reason for his insistence that payroll taxes be described as "contributions" was to foster the impression that the program's resources represented money held in trust for its beneficiaries. "With those taxes in there, no damn politician can ever scrap my social security program," he said.

FDR's widely quoted hex worked well. His 1936 election opponent, Alf Landon, was the first politician, but not the last, to learn the hard way that attacking Social Security was a recipe for defeat. While destiny may have dictated Barry Goldwater's landslide loss to Lyndon Johnson in the 1964 presidential race, his proposal to make Social Security voluntary—which smelled to voters like a plan to kill it—didn't help. When a Reagan administration proposal to slash benefits sent 26 incumbent Republican congressmen to defeat in the 1982 midterm elections, the program's reputation as the "third rail" of American politics was confirmed.

That electoral rout spurred libertarian enemies of the program to undertake a round of deep thinking. The following year, a privatization blueprint written by two analysts at the Heritage Foundation, Stuart Butler and Peter Germanis, surfaced in the libertarian Cato Institute's *Cato Journal.* Mischievously entitled "Achieving a 'Leninist' Strategy," the article observed that while Social Security was certain to collapse someday under its own fiscal burdens, it was worth examining the Bolshevik leader's precept that even a preordained revolution often needs to be jump-started by an elite vanguard.

Butler and Germanis argued that as long as the public remained convinced that Social Security would reliably provide their money's worth upon retirement, any politician who toyed with the program would face the same fate as Congress's involuntary 1982 retirees. The key to securing reform, they said, was to "cast doubt on the picture of reality" promoted by Social Security's supporters. This required "guerrilla warfare against both the current Social Security system, and the coalition that supports it."

The theme of a permanent fiscal "crisis" in Social Security emerged soon afterward in the literature of privatization. The program's enemies portrayed the funding crisis of the 1980s, when the system came within months of insolvency, as the harvest of a fundamental flaw in its pay-as-you-go structure, through which the contributions of each generation of workers pay for the benefits of current retirees.

A package of far-reaching reforms in 1983, which adapted the system to changes in American demographics by raising the retirement age and payroll tax rates, fueled this argument by shaking the public's faith in Social Security's long-term stability. By 1984, the program was being slandered as a "Ponzi scheme" by editorialists at the *Wall Street Journal,* using the term for a financial scam that pays off early investors with money extracted from subsequent marks.

Although the 1983 reforms did in fact succeed in stabilizing the program's fiscal condition for several decades, the drumbeat grew more insistent. It soon proved effective: doubts were mounting among younger workers about whether the program would still exist when they were ready for retirement. Those doubts were interpreted, in turn, as proof that the program indeed had an uncertain future.

The payoff of this circular reasoning came in 1994, with the infamous UFO poll.

A "flagship for the presumption that confidence in Social Security has collapsed," the survey of 18- to 34-year-olds commissioned by Third Millennium, a political lobbying group claiming to represent the youthful Generation X, purported to show that the young generation was more likely to believe in UFOs than that Social Security would survive until their own retirement age.

This imagery was too colorful for the press to ignore. *Time* used it as the peg for a cover story on Social Security in 1995 ("You know a government program is in trouble when it's less credible than a flying saucer"). It was still a popular image in 2004 and 2005, cited as fact by the political commentator Chris Matthews as well as Treasury Secretary John Snow.

But the UFO survey was fundamentally misleading. For one thing, it never actually asked people to weigh the relative credibility of UFOs and the survival of Social Security; instead, it asked them to judge the likelihood of each outcome in separate questions. When a similar sample *was* asked in a separate survey to compare the relative likelihood of alien visitors and a future of Social Security benefits, they voted decisively in favor of the latter.

Second, the pollsters were wrong to suggest that their findings demonstrated that public confidence in Social Security had suffered a recent and precipitous collapse. In fact, the public's confidence had been falling for 20 years, since before the 1983 reform. Most important, however, as political scientists Lawrence R. Jacobs and Robert Y. Shapiro have observed, these chronic doubts were irrelevant to, and had never shaken, the public's *support* for Social Security. On the contrary, a series of polls taken between 1984 and 1996 by the National Opinion Research Center consistently demonstrated 90 percent support for the proposition that national spending on Social Security was "about right" or even "too little."

People might not have enough faith that the program would survive, but they wanted it preserved. Privatization advocates who read these results carefully understood that a more sophisticated assault was called for.

Question its relevancy to today's worker

Butler and Germanis proposed a second effective PR weapon against the program: divide and conquer.

"There is a firm coalition behind the present Social Security system," they acknowledged. "Before Social Security can be reformed, we must begin to divide this coalition."

Their plan was to drive a generational wedge into the system's broad base of support by suggesting that the retired and near-retired would reap far better benefits than younger people just entering the workforce. The authors observed that this potent argument was already spreading through the workforce, citing survey results suggesting that an "overwhelming majority" of the young "have stated repeatedly that they have little or no confidence in the present Social Security system."

They also noted, however, that the young weren't devoted voters—unlike the elderly, who could be counted on to turn out in large numbers, especially in any campaign that placed Social Security benefits on the table. Even more worrisome, the political power of the elderly was likely to increase in the future, as the proportion of those over 65 rose from 11.3 percent of the population in 1983 to more than 18 percent in 2030.

Their strategy for neutralizing the powerful senior bloc was politically canny. They recommended that reformers pledge to exempt the retired or near-retired from any program changes. "Instead of spreading widespread panic among our elderly, which will only undermine our efforts to reform the system," they wrote, "we should acknowledge the system's liabilities [that is, the embedded cost of current benefits] as a total writeoff." With the elderly bought off and the young "informed about the problems inherent in the current system. . . . Discontentment will only grow."

It wasn't long before this developed into what economist James Tobin called "an ugly intergenerational conflict" underlying the political debate on Social Security finance. "Many young people," he observed, "regard the system as bankrupt, as budget-busting, and as catering to the self-interest of an affluent retired middle class."

Tobin considered this attitude to be "not well informed." Although "the young evidently expect to support their seniors by heavy payroll taxes and get little or nothing of value in their turn," he wrote, "both official projections and those of private experts show that despite its problems the system can deliver the promised benefits."

But the press picked up the idea and ran with it. *Time,* in the same article that led with the UFO yarn, articulated the injustice in colloquial terms. "If the system let earlier retirees make out like bandits," it reported, "for everyone who follows it's hands up."

The Butler-Germanis prescription to divide young from old has had lasting appeal. It's an integral element of almost every Bush speech about Social Security reform. Within minutes of starting his January 11 event, he reassured the audience "if you're a senior receiving your Social Security check, nothing is going to change. . . . There is plenty of money in the system today to take care of those who have retired or near retirement." Then he added this obligatory rider: "The issue is really for younger folks."

Nevertheless, the evidence for the so-called generational divide in levels of support of Social Security is questionable. While it does appear that younger workers feel greater doubts about the system's future, the statistics don't show lower *sup-*

port for the program in that age group than among the elderly. Interestingly, Butler and Germanis didn't claim that there *was* lower support for Social Security among the young; their idea was to exploit the younger generation's doubts to sap their support, a process they acknowledged would require much time and effort.

Bewail its effect on worker behavior and the overall economy

One of the most cherished precepts of Social Security's critics is that the prospect of a guaranteed retirement stipend discourages families from acting responsibly and saving for retirement themselves. Harvard economist Martin Feldstein, one of the patriarchs of privatization, even tried to calculate the precise dimensions of what he called the "substitution" effect; his conclusion was that every extra dollar of Social Security wealth replaces 50 cents of private savings. (As one journalist wrote acidly of the notion that people would prudently save more if Social Security didn't exist, "This may be true of economists, but what about the rest of us?")

This claim that Social Security encourages a sort of financial sloth hearkens back to the principle of self-reliance, so prevalent in early American philosophy, and to the connection in popular thought between hard work and personal success. But it fails to acknowledge how decisively the principle was ruptured by the experience of the Depression, which taught instead that rich and poor alike may fall victim to what Franklin D. Roosevelt called "the hazards and vicissitudes of life."

*   *   *

In the years since Butler and Germanis published their "Leninist" blueprint, Social Security's enemies have deployed all three arguments so effectively that the idea that the program faces a crisis has become a dismal article of faith for the millions of Americans who pay Social Security taxes and expect someday to collect benefits.

The great danger of a crisis of confidence in Social Security's stability is that it can become a self-fulfilling prophecy. A public convinced that its money is almost certain to be lost is more likely to withdraw its support for the system, to accept draconian prescriptions for reform, and to transfer its confidence to nostrums such as privatization.

By declaring the collapse of the system to be imminent and the need for reform desperate, Social Security's enemies hope to push through a dramatic change in the system before the public has time to recognize that the reforms will make their retirements less secure, not more so; that the costs of their investments will be higher, not lower; and that the basis for legislation that will change the program forever is not fairness, economics, or fiscal responsibility, but ideology.

Chapter Two

The Cornerstone

This law, too, represents a cornerstone in a structure which is being built . . . a law that will take care of human needs and at the same time provide for the United States an economic structure of vastly greater soundness.

—Franklin Delano Roosevelt,
August 14, 1935

ROOSEVELT was a reluctant warrior on behalf of the policy he extolled so fulsomely upon signing the Social Security Act that August Wednesday in 1935. In 1930, as governor of New York, he had strongly campaigned for a social insurance program. But as president five years later, according to one of his biographers, he all but "gagged" at the nature of the program he was asked to send to Congress.

Roosevelt's objections were to the scale of the program and to its initial funding, which required an appropriation from the federal government to supplement the contributions of covered workers. His road map for a social insurance program started with unemployment insurance, added old-age benefits much later, and finally came around to a form of universal health coverage.

So it's perhaps unsurprising that, as the program made its way through the councils of the Roosevelt administration and then through Congress, it often seemed on the verge of being strangled at birth. There were moments at which FDR appeared to brand it with the "kiss of death," as one early proponent moaned after a presidential conference. At another point it seemed destined to die in congressional committee for want of administration support.

But in the end it emerged in a form very near to the Social Security system we have today. From time to time, Roosevelt may have been uneasy with its provisions and its cost, but when its enemies mounted their first scurrilous attacks on the program, he defended it with all the fire and persuasiveness in his verbal arsenal. As a result, Social Security is regarded to this day as the signal domestic achievement of his administration, the epitome of the New Deal.

The program's pedigree as a Depression baby has always been its glory and its burden. For 70 years it has symbolized how the country pulled together to lift some of its most disadvantaged citizens out of poverty during the deepest economic crisis of the twentieth century. But the compromises that were necessary to turn an ideal of liberal democracy into a working program saddled it with many inadequacies that persist to this day, including a regressive tax structure and enormous debt.

Social Security's creators knew their offspring was imperfect. Forced to choose between a flawed program and no program at all, they opted for the former. To understand how their compromises produced the Social Security that we have inherited, it's useful to travel back to the America of the time of its birth.

By the reckoning of professional economists, the business contraction that launched the Great Depression had run its course by the end of 1933. Conditions improved from that point on, but the economic expansion was so slow and meager as to be almost imperceptible. In 1935 a profound pall still lay over the country.

Americans were still picking through the economic wreckage. Unemployment had peaked in 1932 at 25 percent of the workforce—and closer to 38 percent among nonfarm workers. The stock market crash of 1929 may have directly harmed a relatively small segment of citizens, but thousands of banks and savings and loan associations had also closed their doors, extinguishing billions of dollars of deposits belonging to ordinary workers and their families.

The devastation was especially vicious for the elderly. Among men over 65 who were looking for work, the unemployment rate was 54 percent. Another 25 percent were nominally still employed but temporarily laid off. Nor were people their age a marginal segment of the population. The proportion of Americans older than 60 had doubled in the first three decades of the century. They were, naturally, prone to illness and injury, less employable than other workers, generally needier. Adding to their embitterment was the unfathomability of the collapse in fortunes that had struck them. They had spent their lives honoring the American promise—working hard, saving money, building the nation—and just as they neared retirement they were cast out of work and deprived of their savings. Many of those who had counted on pensions from their employers were further disenfranchised, for the Depression had wiped out thousands of pension plans, too. Public old-age programs that might have helped take up the slack existed in only a handful of states, and those provided scarcely enough money to subsist on.

One saving grace was that the traditional family safety net had not yet become entirely frayed by urbanization. Younger generations had not ceased to accept their responsibility to care for their elders in ways dictated by the customs and rhythms of the prevailing agrarian economy. But for many families, the loss of resources caused by the Depression had made such obligations nearly unsupportable. Families faced options that they could never have imagined, much less considered, only a few years earlier. Appeals for government assistance poured into the White House by the hundreds in letters such as this one, addressed to "President Franklin D. Roosevelt, Washington, D.C," by a Texas widow on behalf of her aged mother:

"She is helpless, suffering from Sugar Diabetes, which has affected her mind. She has to be cared for in the same manner as an infant. She is out of funds completely. Her son whom she used to keep house for is in a hospital in Waco, Texas—no compensation for either himself or her. . . . I appeal to you to place your dear mother in my dear mother's place—With no money and no place to go unless it be to the poor house."

Among the industrialized nations, the United States stood alone in its lack of a social insurance program protecting workers and their families from the miseries of illness, injury, old-age, or destitution. The world's first national medical care program had been launched by Germany in 1883 under Otto von Bismarck, who proceeded to add workers' compensation, survivor benefits, and old-age coverage. The rest of the industrialized world soon followed. In 1935, when the United States was first coming to grips with the need for a public assistance program for outcasts from the industrial revolution, similar programs already existed in Great Britain, France, Belgium, Canada, Denmark, Finland, Norway, Sweden, Spain, Russia, Switzerland, and the Netherlands, as well as in many countries that we still deem part of the third world today.

There are many reasons why the idea of social insurance was late taking root in the United States. One cause is certainly the cherished precept of "rugged individualism," a philosophical strain unique to this country and related to the predilection for laissez-faire capitalism. Another reason may have been the absence of a strong socialist threat like that in Germany, where Bismarck had instituted his broad social program in part to take the wind out of the leftists' sails.

For all that, the concept of public assistance was not entirely alien to these shores. It could not be found at the federal level, but 44 states had launched workers' compensation programs in some form by 1935, and 24 provided old-age pensions. They included New York, where Governor Franklin D. Roosevelt had himself established a program funded by worker contributions. Many such programs were implemented haphazardly, however. Sometimes they required individual counties to opt in or were subject to rigorous and demeaning means-testing that discouraged even the most destitute applicants. Often they were baldly manipulative: in Louisiana the pensions of black men were halved during the summer harvest to hustle them back to the cotton fields to work.

Unemployment insurance spread much more rapidly among the states, with programs in Wisconsin and Ohio regarded as models for their breadth and creativity. As New York's governor, Roosevelt was among the supporters of mandatory unemployment too, a position he carried into the White House.

But the idea of a comprehensive federal program of social insurance lived largely in the hearts of a clutch of progressive reformers—that is, until a series of social movements spread across the country like a prairie fire and forced the idea onto the national agenda.

One of the first such movements to gain widespread attention was founded by Francis E. Townsend, a 66-year-old retired physician in Long Beach, California. Townsend, a gaunt man with a shock of white hair, had spent the first part of his professional career practicing medicine in North Dakota, until health problems sent him packing for southern California. There he dabbled in what was already the regional craze of real estate speculation. But he also spent enough hours practicing in a public health office to witness the human toll of the Depression firsthand. When he lost his city job in 1933, he became part of the toll himself.

The founding legend of the Townsend movement says that one morning later that year he looked out his window at an alley strewn with rubbish barrels and noticed "three haggard, very old women, stooped with great age, bending over the barrels, clawing into the contents." The sight goaded the normally soft-spoken Townsend into a flight of profane invective, which he directed not at the women, but at the social conditions that had brought them so low.

Drawing on the training he had received in medical school from a socialist-leaning professor and his own reading of Edward Bellamy's early socialist tract *Looking Backward: 2000–1887,* Townsend conceived an anti-poverty program and outlined it in a letter to the *Long Beach Press-Telegram.* The essence of his platform (as he later refined it) was the payment of a monthly grant of $200 to every citizen over 60, the money to be spent within 30 days. The program would be financed by a 2 percent tax on all commercial transactions, an inelegant and highly regressive system that would subject goods to multiple taxes as they moved through production and distribution to the final purchaser.

Even by the standards of the time, Townsend's proposal was impracticably generous. The $200 stipend in 1934, much larger than most potential recipients had ever received in wages, would be worth more than $2,900 in today's dollars. If 10 million people signed up, the annual outflow would be $24 billion, or about 40 percent of the country's gross domestic product at the time.

Townsend dismissed such cavils by arguing that the very point of his plan was to stimulate economic demand by putting lots of cash in people's pockets. In any event, such detailed analysis soon became irrelevant, for the Townsend plan was being taken up with religious zeal across the country. More than 5,000 Townsend Clubs, with 2 million members, had been established by the end of 1934, forming what historian Kenneth S. Davis aptly described as "the first effective pressure group for the elderly ever organized in America." Movement gatherings took on the atmosphere of evangelical camp meetings, led by preachers and punctuated by hymn singing and personal testimony. The meetings ended with a refashioned version of "Onward, Christian Soldiers": "Onward, Townsend soldiers, marching as to war...." In January 1935, the elements of Townsend's plan reached the House of Representatives, where they were cobbled into a bill and introduced by John S. McGroarty, 72, a conservative Democrat from California.

As the Townsend movement was spreading from the West, a more practiced professional politician in the South was building his own movement upon the foundation of nationwide economic discontent.

Huey Long had been elected to the U.S. Senate as a Louisiana Democrat in 1930 and had broken with Roosevelt by 1933, apparently over their mutual distaste for each other's political tactics—roughnecked intimidation on Long's side, canny persuasion on FDR's. But Long did have a visceral feel for the resentments inspired in the common American worker by the concentration of capital.

In launching his Share the Wealth plan in 1932, Long, whose written manifesto was entitled *Every Man a King,* proposed granting a free college education to all, a homestead allowance of $5,000 to every family, a government-guaranteed annual income of $2,000, and a pension for everyone over 60. Rather than finance his scheme with a national transaction tax, as Townsend proposed, Long played on, even stoked, his followers' animosity toward plutocrats. The money for Share the Wealth would come from millionaires—through the confiscation of all income over $1 million and all fortunes larger than $5 million.

Long's plan lacked even Townsend's patchwork economic rationale. It was all about punishing the wealthy and appropriating their leisured lifestyle. The historian Arthur Schlesinger called Share the Wealth, harshly, "a hillbilly's paradise—$5,000 capital endowment without work, a radio, washing machine, automobile in every home."

Yet Long accurately perceived the injustice embedded in the distribution of wealth in the United States. By 1935, the crusade he had launched under the banner of the Share Our Wealth Society claimed 7 million members. Today's historians consider the figure to be a wild exaggeration, but the movement was certainly large enough to make mainstream politicians uneasy, even more so when the Louisiana Kingfish began to talk of organizing a third political party and challenging Roosevelt for the presidency in 1936. When traditionally stalwart Democratic constituents such as union members started joining Share Our Wealth clubs, one of FDR's advisers warned him: "It is symptoms like these I think we should watch very carefully."

There was more to keep their eyes on. The third major popular movement for social insurance was another California phenomenon, this one headed by the great muckraking author Upton Sinclair. After a career writing bestsellers such as *The Jungle,* a classic exposé of the meatpacking industry, Sinclair had settled in Beverly Hills. Three times he had run for statewide office on the Socialist Party ticket; three times he had lost. But in 1933, urged on by a wealthy Democratic supporter, he announced he would seek the Democratic nomination for governor. Sinclair's manifesto was a pamphlet entitled *I, Governor of California and How I Ended Poverty: A True Story of the Future.* His program was known as the EPIC plan, for "End Poverty in California."

Sinclair proposed that the state buy or lease idle industrial plants and turn them over to cooperatives of unemployed workers. The workers would manufacture the goods they needed for themselves and trade any surplus with other co-ops, forming a closed but expanding circle. Sinclair also planned to repeal the state sales tax in favor of an inheritance tax, a property tax, and a progressive income tax.

The renowned author's candidacy brought the national spotlight to California to a degree that would not be seen again until a movie star's campaign 70 years later. In the 1934 Democratic primary, Sinclair sailed to victory over eight opponents, a feat that won him an invitation to the Roosevelt family retreat at Hyde Park, New York. The president's advisers endorsed him and his statewide Democratic ticket gingerly, but FDR himself greeted Sinclair warmly and started paying close attention to the political fortunes of the EPIC plan. EPIC was an experiment, he reasoned, but even failed experiments often taught valuable lessons.

Sinclair rode a wave of popular fascination for a few months, then got caught in the undertow. His personal and philosophical eccentricities proved rich fodder for his opponents. The Republican establishment fabricated slanders against him, even enlisting Hollywood studios—whose bosses were no more eager than other wealthy businessmen to have a radical governor seated in Sacramento—to concoct fake newsreels depicting a tide of bums and hobos heading for California, supposedly lured across the state line by Sinclair's utopian promises. California Democrats, and ultimately the White House, backed away. Upon losing the election to a colorless Republican opponent, Sinclair promptly produced a campaign postmortem entitled *I, Candidate for Governor: And How I Got Licked.*

To Roosevelt, EPIC's meteoric appeal was a reminder that the persistent pain of the Depression had made the country ripe for social agitators. Some of them were rather less dignified than Townsend and Sinclair. From the Midwest, Father Charles E. Coughlin built a radio following with a populist, anticapitalist pitch uttered in a soothing baritone flavored with a trace of Irish brogue (though he had been born in Canada).

By 1935 Coughlin's rhetoric had becoming increasingly intemperate, combining economic discontent, isolationist fervor, and anti-Semitism into diatribes against Communists, international bankers, labor unions—and Franklin D. Roosevelt.

The president needed to get in front of the parade.

＊　　＊　　＊

The kernel of the Social Security Act can be found in a message Roosevelt sent to Congress on June 8, 1934, in which he set forth a broad plan for social insurance that would provide people with "some safeguard against misfortunes which cannot be wholly eliminated in this man-made world of ours." The program, FDR said, would provide "security against the hazards and vicissitudes of life"—specifically, unemployment and old age.

Three weeks later Roosevelt created a Committee on Economic Security under the chairmanship of his legendary secretary of labor, Frances Perkins, and charged it with drafting the necessary legislation. From the start, the committee members found themselves thrashing out issues of social policy that had never been addressed at the federal level before: whether the program should be voluntary or mandatory; funded from individual contributions or general government funds; one that favored the lower-paid over the wealthy; served only the destitute; provided a wholly adequate stipend or merely supplemental assistance; and so on.

Some of these issues were settled in fairly short order; others have remained unresolved for 70 years and still fuel ideological attacks on Social Security today. The committee members, for example, agreed at an early stage to fund the old-age program through contributions from employees and employers. The idea was to avoid means-testing, a demeaning process that stigmatized its subjects as failures but that would probably have to be implemented to control the cost of a program funded from general revenues. Putting the elderly through the ordeal of proving that they were poor enough to receive assistance violated the committee's sense that people were struggling in the 1930s because of systemic, not personal, failure.

Roosevelt himself believed that any federal old-age program should be contributory, like the system he had established in New York. Despite his liberal reputation, Roosevelt was not a fan of welfare programs that involved outright transfers of wealth from rich to poor, and he would be quick to condemn any such proposal as "the same old dole under a new name."

In fact, the committee members were not entirely confident that FDR would support any pension program at all as part of a social insurance package. As was his custom when it came to policy details, he had been sending mixed signals. His June 1934 message appeared to endorse unequivocally a federal old-age program, but only a few months later, while the Committee on Economic Security was drafting its legislation, he shocked the audience at a White House conference by openly doubting that the time was right "for any federal legislation on old-age security." When his remarks ignited a newspaper firestorm, he backtracked again, sending Frances Perkins out to assure reporters that anyone who thought the president had any doubts about an old-age program was certainly mistaken.

In preparing legislation for introduction in early 1935, the committee made several choices that would establish Social Security's form for decades to come.

For one thing, they opted to pay benefits on a sliding scale derived, if loosely, from a worker's career earnings. By doing so they rejected the alternative of a flat rate independent of earnings, which would have involved a much more substantial redistribution of wealth and was seen as penalizing skilled workers in favor of the unskilled.

The committee also rejected a strict pay-as-you-go formula, in which all benefits would be funded by current contributions without any subsidy from the federal budget. The reason was that such a structure would require the system to accumulate a large reserve before any benefits were paid, unless the stipends in the first several years were to be pointlessly meager. But putting off benefits for more than five or six years would leave thousands of poverty-stricken senior citizens—whose plight had inspired the legislation, after all—without aid. If one of the rationales for the program was to erode the appeal of grassroots movements like Townsend's and Long's, a lengthy delay in paying pensions would defeat its purpose.

The drafters' solution to this conundrum was a hybrid financing scheme. Initially the program was to be funded exclusively through a payroll tax set at 1 percent of earnings, split 50-50 between workers and their employers, beginning in mid-1937. Monthly benefits would not begin until 1942. By that point there would be enough money in the reserve to pay significant benefits, but insofar as the first cohorts of beneficiaries would have been making contributions for only a few years, they would be receiving far greater sums than they had actually put into the fund.

Because the scheduled benefits would draw down the reserve pool to a dangerously shallow level once workers began retiring in large numbers, the federal government would intervene in the mid-1950s to provide whatever subsidy was needed to establish a comfortable long-term reserve of $11 billion. From that point on, the system would be self-sustaining.

This arrangement has fostered confusion and ridicule ever since. Labeling the payroll tax a "contribution" has encouraged people to misconstrue Social Security as a form of conventional insurance, as though every worker pays directly for his or her own retirement, and to overlook its function of providing a broad social safety net to keep even the lowest-paid citizens out of poverty in old age. The system's critics regularly portray this terminology as a fraud on the public: "The Founders 'sold' Social Security to the people, and to Congress, as a system of insurance," complained Dorcas R. Hardy, a former Social Security commissioner turned privatization advocate, in a 1991 book deploring the Social Security "mess." (It's debatable whether most people are as misled as Hardy and her fellow privateers suggest.)

One final hitch arose before the introduction of the Social Security bill. At the last minute, Treasury Secretary Henry Morgenthau Jr., who had participated in its drafting as a member of the committee, confessed to FDR his uneasiness that the program was too flimsily financed. He was especially remorseful about burdening a future Congress with the responsibility for truing up the reserve fund.

At his urging, several changes were made in the bill: The contribution rate was doubled, to 1 percent each from workers and employers. The reach of the system was reined in by excluding farm workers, transient laborers, and domestic help—ironically, leaving uncovered precisely those workers who "had the least economic security and were the most ruthlessly exploited," as one historian wrote later. The changes were designed to enable the system to build a reserve of $47 billion by 1980, without the government's contributing a cent from general revenues.

Once introduced, the bill drew fire from both ends of the political spectrum. The left damned it as inadequate and a big step back from the comprehensive program Roosevelt had outlined a year earlier. The right attacked it, as the historian Kenneth S. Davis wrote, "on the usual grounds that it would discourage thrift, encourage shiftlessness, destroy individual initiative, and in general raise hell with the moral character of the citizenry and the workings of the economy"—a bill of indictment remarkably similar to that advanced by many of the program's enemies today.

Despite these objections, the Social Security Act passed easily in Congress and was signed promptly by FDR on August 14, 1935. As the product of a committee and the congressional wringer, it was a patchwork quilt with plenty for everyone to denigrate. The New Deal historian William Leuchtenburg, writing in 1963, labeled it "an astonishingly inept and conservative piece of legislation." It lacked provisions for unemployment coverage and health care, despite Roosevelt's promises, and denied coverage to the neediest workers. "In no other welfare system in the world," Leuchtenburg observed, "did the state shirk all responsibility for old-age indigence and insist that funds be taken out of the current earnings of workers. By relying on regressive taxation and withdrawing vast sums to build up reserves, the act did untold economic mischief."

Still, as he acknowledged, the act was a landmark in American law, reversing "historic assumptions about the nature of social responsibility." For the first time, the nation recognized that the common people whose labor contributed so much to the national wealth—a contribution almost never acknowledged—deserved a dignified retirement free from want.

It would not be long before the program's enemies regrouped for their first campaign to kill the system.

In two terms as governor of Kansas, Alf Landon had built a reputation as a moderate Republican. He had enacted conservation programs, reduced utility rates, implemented an unemployment program and an income tax, and even pushed enabling legislation for several New Deal programs—including Social Security—through the state legislature. His speech accepting the GOP nomination for the presidency in 1936 conveyed almost none of the rancor toward Franklin Roosevelt that infected the party platform.

But like other conservatives, he was unhappy with Social Security's financing scheme, particularly with the size of the reserve, which critics viewed as a giant slush fund. Republicans were already suspicious of Roosevelt's imperial presidency; if he and his successors got their hands on the program's money, they feared, the federal government would acquire an unprecedented ability to undertake programs and projects with nationwide reach.

In the heat of a presidential campaign, such issues were perhaps destined to be simplified to the point of caricature. And Social Security could not be insulated from the election. As the campaign heated up in September 1936, Landon, a dull speaker, was having difficulty stirring his audiences to even the semblance of enthusiasm. "Desperately in search of an electrifying issue," he decided to focus on the program, which was still so young that the first payroll tax deductions were still more than three months away.

Speaking in Milwaukee, Landon abruptly launched an attack on Social Security as "unjust, unworkable, stupidly drafted, and wastefully financed." The payroll tax, he said, was "a cruel hoax" and "a fraud on the working man." He portrayed the system's need for complicated record keeping as the harbinger of a police state. "The Republican Party," he proclaimed, "will have nothing to do with any plan that involves prying into the personal records of 26 million people."

What followed was the GOP's first concerted assault on the program, the first attempt to make it an issue in a national election, and the first appearance of tactics that were, as historian Davis noted, "ruthlessly disregardful of truth and decency."

A mere week before Election Day, industrial workers across

the country found printed notices in their pay envelopes warning that, starting January 1, their employers would be "compelled by a Roosevelt 'New Deal' law" to deduct 1 percent from their wages. The flyers suggested that the employees might never see any return from the deduction; the material, provided by the Republican National Committee to compliant employers, deliberately made no mention of the program the deductions were designed to support. *"You're Sentenced* TO A WEEKLY PAY REDUCTION for ALL OF YOUR WORKING LIFE," read one particularly florid flyer. "YOU'LL HAVE TO *SERVE THE SENTENCE* UNLESS YOU HELP TO REVERSE IT NOV. 3, ELECTION DAY."

On the stump, meanwhile, Landon fleshed out his theme of the program's intrusiveness by suggesting that enrollees might be fingerprinted, subjected to mug shots, or forced to wear ID tags around their necks. On the very eve of the election, Hearst newspapers obligingly published on their front pages a photograph of a man wearing a tag on a chain under the headline: DO YOU WANT A TAG AND A NUMBER IN THE NAME OF FALSE SECURITY?

The newly organized Social Security board, still struggling with the challenge of assembling a staff and developing an administrative system for an unprecedented and unique program, happened by pure luck to be well positioned to mount a defense.

Having decided to start assigning account numbers in mid-November, after the election—specifically to avoid giving the program's enemies a pretext to make a campaign issue of the necessary formalities—the board had already distributed 50 million pamphlets to labor unions, explaining the program to their members—"literature telling what a wonderful act this was," recalled Arthur J. Altmeyer, who had been appointed Social Security's first director. Altmeyer instructed the unions not to hold back the pamphlets until the original target date of November 15. Instead, they were to place them immediately in the hands of their members at the factory gates.

In the end, the first major assault on Social Security turned into its enemies' first failure. Roosevelt, the ambivalent champion of federal old-age benefits, was stirred to deliver in the program's defense what many regard as one of his greatest political speeches. Speaking before an exhilarated crowd at New York's Madison Square Garden on October 31, he pilloried the Republicans for their attack on the social safety net.

"Only desperate men with their backs to the wall would descend so far below the level of decent citizenship to foster the current pay-envelope campaign against America's working people," he said. "Every message in a pay envelope, even if it is the truth, is a command to vote according to the will of the employer. But this propaganda is worse—it is deceit."

Then he issued a warning that would echo down the decades. When the Republicans imply that the reserve funds accumulated by the system "will be stolen by some future Congress, diverted to some wholly foreign purpose," he said, "they attack the integrity and honor of the American government itself."

It was as though he foresaw the attacks that would emerge 70 years later.

Alf Landon lost the 1936 election in a historic landslide. He later called his assault on Social Security his biggest campaign blunder, for it had stirred the electorate to render a decisive vote expressing hope and optimism for the program. In staving off the threat, Social Security gave politicians the first hint that there was something about it the American people considered very special.

But its victory would be temporary.

Chapter Three

The Legacy of Ida May Fuller

T HE PHOTOGRAPHS SHOW a pleasantly moon-faced old lady in wire-rim spectacles and a floral print frock. Local history says she was known as "Aunt Ida" to the residents of the rural Vermont precincts where she was born in 1874 and died a full century later. To the Social Security Administration, she was the recipient of the very first monthly retirement check it ever issued, number 00-000-001.

Ida May Fuller worked as a legal secretary and a schoolteacher, earning a monthly wage of $75. She never married and had no children. Like some 40 million other working Americans, in January 1937 she began paying a 1 percent tax out of her wages to fund the new system of national social insurance. The levy on her earnings came to 75 cents, matched by her employer nickel for nickel. By October 1939, when she retired, her contributions had tallied to $24.75. When check number 00-000-001 was issued to her on January 31, 1940, the sum was $22.54.

It was a modest amount even then—$296 in today's dollars—but Ida May Fuller would eventually live to the age of 100. When she died in 1975, her $24.75 in taxes had yielded benefits totaling $22,888.92.

For her contemporaries and the first generations that followed her into retirement, Fuller's experience symbolized the promise of Social Security, a fulfillment of America's commitment to granting its citizens an unburdened old age. On such major program anniversaries as its twentieth in 1955, news photographers would gather at her home to snap a few commemorative shots. Obligingly she would repeat, for the umpteenth time, the story of how she had dropped in at a government office in Rutland one November day in 1939 to inquire whether she was due a retirement pension. "It wasn't that I expected anything, mind you, but I knew I'd been paying for something called Social Security and I wanted to ask the people in Rutland about it."

For Social Security's critics, especially those who beat the privatization drum, the mismatch of payments and benefits in Aunt Ida's Social Security file symbolizes something very different: the ripoff of the young by the old. Recall *Time*'s plaint: "If the system let earlier retirees make out like bandits, for everyone who follows it's hands up." These critics believe that Social Security's fundamental flaw was etched into the system from the day of its enactment. To them, Fuller's legacy to later generations is crushing debt.

The so-called legacy debt is indeed a continuing—and expanding—artifact of Congress's original decision to pay the first Social Security recipients greater benefits than their meager contributions warranted. Depending on how it is measured and over what time frame, the legacy debt can be calculated today at as much as $10.4 trillion in present value. This number, while misleading as a metric of the system's current financial condition, is at least a useful reminder that Social Security's future is inextricably tied to its past.

The liberal benefits granted to the first retirees resulted from a compromise designed to allow meaningful payments to be made to workers who had contributed taxes for only a few years. The designers of Social Security could not accept the irony that the system they were creating in response to the suffering of contemporary senior citizens might actually leave them in the lurch. (The members of what we are pleased to call the "greatest generation" still exert a pull on the more history-minded of today's Social Security experts. "Younger workers should remember that they did not have to live through two world wars and a depression," says Edward M. Gramlich, a Federal Reserve System governor with an enduring interest in Social Security reform.)

The original 1935 legislation called for Social Security to start collecting payroll taxes in 1937, but not to make monthly disbursements until 1942. Only four years after enacting the program, Congress overwhelmingly passed the first set of enhancements. Characteristically generous, the 1939 amendments added dependents' benefits for the spouses and underaged children of retired workers, as well as survivor benefits for the immediate families of deceased workers. All benefit amounts were increased from the levels set in 1935, and the start of monthly payments was accelerated by two years, to 1940.

These changes saddled the program with increased start-up liabilities. The principal beneficiaries of this increased largesse were the first generations of retirees. The Social Security Administration has calculated that the 1875 cohort—that is, the group of all recipients born that year—received an average annual rate of return on their contributions of more than 35 percent, obviously the best average return of any age group. For those who lived to an unusually late age, such as Ida May Fuller, the return was even higher. Somewhat counterbalancing that figure is the fact that relatively few Americans born in the 1870s reached retirement age at all. (The average life expectancy at birth for a male in that era was less than 40; even 20-year-olds lived only to an average age of 60.) Moreover, the absolute benefit was relatively small.

Because Social Security was designed as a pay-as-you-go system, in which current retirement benefits are paid from the contributions of current workers, this transfer of resources from young to old continued for several decades. All those born from 1875 through 1935 received greater benefits than could have been financed from their own contributions. This increased the legacy debt because the shortfall was made up from the contributions of younger workers.

These generational transfers peaked for beneficiaries who were born between 1910 and 1916, a group that retired between 1975 and 1981. The last retirees to receive more on average from Social Security than they had paid in was the 1935 cohort—Americans who were born during the tail end of the Great Depression, spent their childhoods in a nation at war, and reached their full retirement age in 2000. Thanks to higher tax rates and benefit adjustments enacted in 1983, everyone born in 1936 and later will, on average, pay more in taxes than they receive in benefits as expressed in present value, with the excess payments essentially being applied to help pay down the legacy debt. As the economists Peter Diamond and Peter Orszag observe, in practical terms this results in their rate of return on contributions falling below prevailing market interest rates.

That's not the same as saying that all those born after 1935 will lose money under Social Security. As Henry J. Aaron and Robert D. Reischauer have noted, the payroll taxes paid by the later generations are sufficient to pay for all the old age, disability, and survivor and dependents benefits they and their families will receive. Although their rate of return may be lower than their forebears', they are contributing to a system that provides them with a guaranteed lifetime inflation-adjusted annuity, at an implicit cost that is a fraction of what is charged by retail investment firms to convert lump-sum assets into long-term annuities, along with disability and survivor benefits that would be costly to obtain in the commercial market. Social Security shields workers from many of the pitfalls that exist in private pension systems, including the risk that corporate sponsors will fail or that inflation or market downturns will erode the value of their vested pensions.

Still, understanding how the early-generation transfers depress today's rate of return will also give us an understanding of some of the peculiarities of Social Security's financing, while illuminating the implications of various reform schemes. Among other things, it will show why the lush returns often forecast for owners of private retirement accounts may be vastly overstated.

To illustrate, let's think of Social Security's legacy debt in terms of an obligation handed down from generation to generation within a single family.

Let's say that years ago your father accumulated a nest egg of $100,000 for his and your mother's retirement. Let's assume that this sum would be enough to support them comfortably in their old age. In other words, it was not only an asset to your parents but to you, because it ensured that their upkeep wouldn't be a burden to your own young family. Imagine, however, that before your parents can spend it for their own retirement, your grandfather falls ill and asks your father for support. Your father accordingly spends his $100,000 on your grandfather. As a result, when his own retirement date arrives, he is bereft of assets and, naturally, turns to you. You withdraw half of the $200,000 that you had saved for your own retirement and pass it back to the previous generation.

What have you given up? Not only the $100,000 in cash, but all the interest that it might have accumulated before your own retirement. If your $200,000 account had remained intact and appreciated at 6 percent a year, then 35 years later you would have owned an account worth more than $1.5 million. Instead you have a bit more than $760,000. Or to put it another way, the rate of return on your original $200,000 has been cut nearly by half.

Within a devoted family, this obligation established in your grandfather's generation would be passed down as a sort of negative heirloom. Although each generation would make the previous one whole—you would repay to your father the money he donated to his father, your children would repay you, and so on—each successive generation would also be deprived of the interest that would have accumulated from the very first reverse bequest. Thanks to the magic of compound interest, moreover, the implicit legacy debt would grow over time. For all anyone would know, your father's initial $100,000 donation could have been the seed of a great family fortune; instead it's the foundation of an inherited liability.

There are very few ways to end this cycle. One generation can refuse to pay its parents' bills, which would render the parents destitute but relieve successive generations of the obligation forever. Alternatively, one generation can pay twice, covering its parents' needs *and* its own without demanding help from its children; henceforth each generation would be free to spend its nest egg on itself. The third way is for successive generations each to pay down a bit of the debt—for instance by paying some, but not all, of their parents' needs. Eventually a generation would be born entirely free of the obligation. Which generation would arrive in this immaculate state would depend on how much of the debt each previous generation had paid down.

Our parable underscores some of the intergenerational responsibilities implicit in Social Security, along with the choices embedded in various proposals for reform.

The sense of duty that led your father to pay his parents' bills might have stemmed not only from habit or custom, but from his appreciation for how much they had sacrificed over their own lives for him—working to put food on the table, imparting moral and social learning, financing the education that enabled him and his offspring to move up the socioeconomic ladder. These were investments by the parents whose returns were reaped by their children. Seen in this light, the retirement contribution might be considered a partial repayment by the children for the parents' expenditures on their behalf.

In a similar way, as Gramlich recognizes, Social Security acknowledges the debt that younger Americans in the 1950s and 1960s owed to their parents and grandparents, who struggled through the Depression and fought or maintained the home front in World War II to secure the postwar world.

More than gratitude and altruism animates this aspect of the program, however; there is also self-interest. By allowing the elderly to live independent lives, the program also relieves their children of the burden of supporting them in more direct fashion. Robert M. Ball, a one-time Social Security commissioner and an advocate of liberal reforms, was only half-joking when he remarked that one reason to support the program was "the value of not having your mother-in-law living with you."

Not only families, but society at large has gained relief through the old-age program. The community has not only a compassionate, but an economic interest in not allowing the aged to "starve and die in the street," as the Nobel Prize–winning economist James Tobin put it: Caring for the destitute through public relief and public health programs is always more expensive than keeping people out of poverty in the first place.

For all that the legacy debt has been exploited by Social Security's enemies to paint a gruesome picture of the program's financial future—it is, after all, the source of President Bush's scary image of an economic drain of more than $10 trillion—our hypothetical family's history should demonstrate that to a certain extent the debt can be carried indefinitely, continually refinanced like a revolving charge card or, indeed, like the national debt.

In the case of Social Security, it is true that under certain circumstances it might be wise to bring the debt under control. It might at some point grow to such a large ratio of the gross domestic product that people come to fear the stability of the economy itself. Has the legacy debt reached that point already? That's doubtful. Projected out to the limitless future, the legacy debt comes to 1.2 percent of GDP. One can debate whether that's a terrible burden or a modest one, but it's certainly a less scary number than $10 trillion.

The legacy debt does, however, help us assess the ramifications of possible policy choices for Social Security's future. For one thing, it provides us with a rationale for two oft-proposed reforms: expanding enrollment in Social Security to state and local government employees (the only sizable group of workers still largely unenrolled in Social Security); and eliminating the cap on taxable earnings in the payroll tax.

As long as state and local government workers remain outside the system, they are exempted from shouldering their share of the legacy debt. This is so even though their own forebears may have been beneficiaries of the early generational transfers, and although they certainly benefit today from the economy for which those generations laid the foundation.

The same is true of those whose earnings exceed the payroll tax cap ($90,000 in 2005). To the extent that their earnings are exempt from Social Security tax, they also evade their full share of the legacy. Raising the tax cap might be interpreted by the anti-tax lobby as a tax increase, but arguably it is no such thing: it's a fair repayment for services rendered by the greatest generation. Spreading the debt burden more broadly and fairly, in any case, will only improve Social Security's fiscal condition.

Another way that our family analogy illuminates the policy choices is by demonstrating the implications of various options for restructuring Social Security.

Every proposal to privatize the program must involve one of the three options for extinguishing the debt (one generation going without, one paying twice, or all sharing the burden). This point is often ignored by privatization advocates, but sophisticated economic analysts aren't fooled. The legacy debt can't simply be wished away. It can be carried forward only as long as the generational transfers continue—which they would be as long as Social Security remains as it is today.

But the moment the program's financing structure changes, the debt, in effect, comes due. As the Congressional Budget Office observed in 2004, "a pay-as-you-go retirement system such as Social Security cannot move to a funded basis—for example, to a system of private retirement accounts—without putting an extra burden on some generation or generations. To move to a funded system in one generation, either workers have to pay double, some generation must receive no benefits, or some balance of increased payments and reduced benefits must occur."

In most privatization plans, this unpleasant reality manifests itself as requirements for sharp benefit cuts, huge subsidies to retirees to be paid from the federal budget, or enormous new federal borrowings. The privatization lobby often lays the blame for these choices on the cost of the baby-boomer retirements, which happen to be imminent, but that's a misrepresentation; in fact the choices arise from the legacy debt.

Benefit cuts are the equivalent of depriving one generation of the transfer from its children. That's because whichever generation was to retire under a new, reduced benefit schedule would already have paid the previous generation's tab through its own payroll taxes—but it wouldn't be receiving as much from the next generation.

If the transition to private accounts, alternatively, were funded by transfers from the federal budget to avoid a benefit reduction, this would amount to charging one generation twice. The generation that received the general-fund transfers would have paid for them through its own income taxes, at the same time it was paying for the previous generation's retirement through its own payroll taxes. Meanwhile, its children would be relieved of the burden of paying for their parents' retirement, because the intergenerational transfers would have come to an end.

The third possibility, spreading the legacy debt among several generations through federal borrowings, might arguably be more fair than either of the previous options, but it still incurs a high cost derived from an acceleration of the legacy repayment: rather than spreading the debt over many generations, it would have to be repaid over the term of the government bonds, probably a mere 30 years.

How does all this apply to the potential rate of return on private retirement accounts? It shows that factoring the legacy debt into the cost of privatizing Social Security must reduce those promised returns substantially. In fact, one team of prominent economists has estimated that paying off the legacy debt would eliminate *all* of the gains from privatization. (This reflects the familiar dictum that "there is no free lunch," in privatization or anywhere else.) In other words, retirees would get roughly the same risk-adjusted return from private accounts—notwithstanding all the predictions of great profits to be made in the stock market—that they would receive from traditional Social Security.

The real issue in privatization, the economists said, isn't whether there's a long-term gain to be pocketed by all retirees in transitioning to a privatized system. Their conclusion was that there is no gain. All that can be achieved is a shifting of the legacy debt among generations. If we load it onto today's workers, say, by raising taxes or cutting benefits today to fund transition costs, then we are merely relieving the burden on future generations. Today's workers will have less money for retirement so that their children will have more.

The question that needs to be debated, the economists concluded, is "whether this is a tradeoff worth making."

There is one last wrinkle in this issue of cost-shifting frogeneration to generation. The privatization lobby isn't merely thinking about charging the baby boomers twice in order to pay off the legacy cost. It has come up with a way to charge the boomers *three* times. Its method, as we will see, involves some very fancy fakery involving what is known as the Social Security trust fund.

Chapter Four

The Assumption Game

THE BEST THING about mathematics is its rigor. Two plus two equals four, no matter what object is being counted; one dollar enhanced by 6 percent a year will be worth $1.06 a year later, regardless of the weather outside, the force of gravity, or the party controlling the White House.

The worst thing about mathematics is that its rigor runs only skin deep. Introduce even a trivial uncertainty into an equation, and you muddle its relationship to the real world. One dollar enhanced by 6 percent is $1.06, but what if you have only a 1-in-5 chance of obtaining that 6 percent, and a 4-in-5 chance of obtaining 2 percent? What, then, will the dollar be worth in another year? You can't know for sure; you can only express the value as a range of probabilities.

And if you pile uncertainty upon uncertainty, say, by constructing a mathematical formula out of thousands of interrelated factors whose values are only guesses—whose *interrelationships* are guesses—you will still produce a solution that looks real. But what you will have is vapor masquerading as solid rock.

This is a fair description of how the experts arrive at almost all of the most important and oft-cited statistics in the Social Security debate. The projections of the system's increasing costliness and its enormous deficit—figures denominated in trillions of dollars—as well as the forecasts of its looming bankruptcy, are all based on numbers that seem very real. The numbers are compiled annually by the Social Security trustees into estimates of the system's financial health over the next 75 years that are revised every March. (The trustees' 2005 annual report therefore covers the period from 2005 to 2079.) Accepted as articles of faith by Social Security's defenders as well as its enemies, these numbers are the foundation stones of all the leading proposals to save Social Security, as well as those aimed at dismantling it.

But they all arise from a patchwork of conjectures. Some are no more than educated stabs in the dark, while others are derived from sophisticated judgments and computer-generated trend charts. But even the latter are hardly flawless.

These statistics are also subject to change from one year to the next, sometimes dramatically. Drawing solid conclusions from them becomes something of an art form. Consider the prediction, made in the Social Security trustees' 2005 annual report, that the program's trust fund will be tapped out in 2041 because of the rate at which expenses will outrun tax revenues over the next three and a half decades. This date has been repeated so often and so dogmatically during the recent debate over reform that it seems to be etched in stone.

In fact, it has been as variable as the weather. In their 1984 annual report, the Social Security trustees predicted that the fund would run dry in 2063. In the 1995 report, they placed the critical year at 2029. (This would suggest that the system's financial health has improved markedly since that forecast was made.) Meanwhile, the Congressional Budget Office, which employs its own platoon of mathematical wizards, says the trust fund will be sound until at least 2053.

These figures can't all be right. The truth is that the Social Security system's deficit is nothing more than an estimate—an "actuarial construct," as one critic says—highly sensitive to changes in economic variables.

This is not to say that long-range forecasts are useless, only that it's dangerous to rely on them to rationalize dramatic and fundamental long-range changes in the program. That's especially so when these forecasts are so commonly subject to misunderstanding, misinterpretation, and even outright manipulation.

Given the crucial role that statistics play in the debate over Social Security, one might think that the trustees would try to minimize the uncertainties in the formulas they employ. Instead, they have moved in the opposite direction. In 2003, the trustees, a majority of whom were appointed by President Bush, decided to publish for the first time a projection of the system's health not only over the next 75 years, but over *infinity*.

Professional actuaries warned the trustees that the infinite projection would be wildly misunderstood by the public and vulnerable to cynical misuse by ideologues. In this case, for once, the prognosticators were absolutely correct.

The raw numbers from which the trustees generate their long-term projections are developed by the program's Office of the Chief Actuary, a team of highly professional men and women trained in the black art of melding statistical snapshots of the present with piles of historical data into a credible forecast of the program's long-term condition. Despite the aura of magisterial precision enveloping any statistic worked out to two decimal points, the actuarial forecasts are largely gas, although their creators would never characterize them that way. They would prefer to say, in the words of Stephen Goss, Social Security's current chief actuary, that the 75-year forecast harbors "significant uncertainty," and to leave it at that.

One has to delve about one-third of the way into the dense, chart-filled trustees' report—to page 69 of the 2005 edition, to be precise—to find language describing just how spongy their supposedly rigorous forecasts are. There they acknowledge that the projections are based on "inherently uncertain" estimates of "fertility, mortality, immigration, marriage, divorce, productivity, inflation, average earnings, unemployment, retirement, and disability incidence and termination. Other factors are projected using methods that reflect historical and expected future relationships to the basic assumptions. These include total population, life expectancy, labor force, gross domestic product, interest rates, and a myriad of program-specific factors."

These factors, they continue, "are interrelated directly or indirectly . . . [and] these interrelationships can and do change over time." They might have added that many factors can unexpectedly turn on a dime, confounding the expectations of even the wisest economic minds.

As though to underscore their uncertainty, the trustees publish not one forecast, but three. They are labeled "low cost" (that is, best case), "high cost" (worst case), and "intermediate" (middle-of-the-road). In very rough terms the intermediate forecast splits the difference between the two extremes, although the actuaries prefer to say that it represents in their judgment the forecast with the best probability of coming true. Accordingly, by convention the trustees, politicians, ideologues, and other policy mavens concerned with Social Security all treat the intermediate case as the system's more-or-less official estimate.

Recently, the actuaries have started developing what are known as "stochastic" simulations, which involve calculating what happens if hundreds of variables fluctuate randomly throughout the 75-year span. The simulations result in a set of computer-generated graphs illustrating how exponentially more ambiguous the forecasts become as they probe deeper into the future. While the old-fashioned intermediate-case projection in the 2005 report pegged the trust fund's exhaustion date at 2041, for example, the stochastic run constrained the actuaries to reveal that the best they could say with reasonable statistical confidence was that the date would fall somewhere between 2032 and 2065.

Stochastic simulations never get much play in the Social Security debate; in Washington, nobody cares much for ambiguity. The traditional forecasts are much simpler to understand and communicate—an obvious virtue when one is dealing with policy makers who may be long on political power but short on attention span. At an actuarial symposium in 2001, Goss explained that he measured the optimum amount of information that a politician could absorb through "what we call the 'drop' test: if you go to a member of Congress and you give him a piece of paper with a message you need to convey, you put it in front of him for 15 seconds and drop it and you hope he'll be able to tell you what was there."

The real problem with the standard forecasts isn't their simplicity, however, but their inaccuracy. When you scratch the surface of the intermediate projection, you discover that in recent years it has consistently painted an overly pessimistic view of U.S. economic growth, a critical factor in Social Security's finances. By contrast, the so-called low-cost case, which critics generally dismiss as unrealistically Pollyannaish, is the one that has often hit closest to the mark.

Before we examine the evidence for this, we should consider the implications of Social Security forecasts that go seriously awry. The accompanying graph from the 2004 Social Security annual report projects changes in the level of the Social Security trust fund under the three traditional scenarios.

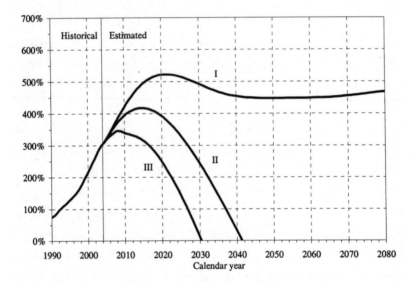

Line II (in the middle) is the intermediate forecast, encompassing the projections of ruin and bankruptcy so beloved by President Bush and the privatization lobby: the trust fund assets rise until roughly 2018 and decline to zero in 2041. At that point, as the president argues in his inelegant phrasing, the system is "flat bust."

Line III, following the worst-case, high-cost scenario, is correspondingly more dire, showing the reserve tapped out more than ten years earlier, in 2030.

Line I, the best-case, low-cost scenario, unsurprisingly paints the sunniest picture: the trust fund crests roughly in 2020, then declines slightly under the burden of baby-boomer retirements before reaching an equilibrium in 2040 that continues off the chart, toward eternity. (The equilibrium level is established at an asset level of nearly 500 percent of annual costs, meaning the trust fund would hold almost enough money to pay benefits five times over.)

According to the low-cost scenario, the trust fund won't be spent down to zero in 2041. But it says more than this: it suggests that the reserve will grow from about $1.6 trillion today to $18 trillion in 2080. In other words, it portrays Social Security's destiny not as insolvency and ruin, but as an embarrassment of riches.

If it really does present the most consistently accurate portrait of the system, then all the expectations of Social Security's collapse are wrong. There may never be a deficit at all.

What evidence is there that the low-cost scenario really is the most accurate? For the answer, we must turn to a man who for the better part of a decade has been hacking his way through the undergrowth of Social Security's actuarial policies as a prophet without honor in his chosen profession.

"I find this work kind of exciting," David Langer told me one winter day from his office in snowbound New York City. "I have a history of being an actuarial sleuth."

The description suits him. For more than ten years, Langer, a dapper, self-confident man of 87 with a shock of silvery hair, an unalterable Brooklyn accent, and a permanently pugnacious expression, has been ruthlessly exposing Social Security's actuarial forecast for the murky crystal ball it is.

A professional actuary whose career has encompassed work for banks, insurance companies, and private clients, Langer started shadowing the Social Security actuaries in 1995. An advisory council appointed by President Clinton was deep into its deliberations over private accounts and other funding alternatives. The conservative campaign to undermine confidence in the program among the young seemed to be bearing fruit: fears that the system wouldn't be there for future generations were heard more and more often.

"I got upset about that sort of attack," Langer recalls. "Having grown up during the Depression, I had an orientation toward social programs." Writing in publications as general as the *Christian Science Monitor* and as technical as *Contingencies*, the official organ of the American Academy of Actuaries, Langer picked apart the actuaries' models. He documented the unwarranted pessimism of the intermediate-case projections, especially in their estimates of economic growth, and showed that the best-case scenario had become a far superior guidepost to the future.

Langer's analyses started to spread to other mainstream publications including the *New York Times,* the *Wall Street Journal,* and *Newsweek.* But he wasn't winning friends at the Social Security Administration. The problem wasn't merely that he was reminding people of the actuaries' fallibility. He had gone further: he was charging that the system's projections were being deliberately manipulated for political ends.

Although the chief actuary's office develops ranges of outcomes for every trend measured in the projections, Langer observed, it is the trustees—all of whom are presidential appointees,

including four cabinet members who sit on the board ex officio—
who select the numbers to be plugged into the three forecasts each
year.

"This is how you cross the border from actuarial science into
politics," he says. In the mid-1990s Langer began to suggest that
the trustees were cooking the forecasts with the actuaries' acqui-
escence, selecting statistics to produce projections advancing their
political goals. He contends that the practice has continued to the
present day. Under a president determined to replace Social Security with private accounts, he contends, the trustees are skewing
their numbers to paint a picture of a system in peril.

Nothing in Langer's oeuvre has caused as much commotion as
this charge. That's hardly surprising, considering that actuaries
pride themselves on being dispassionate compilers of facts and
figures. His assertion that the trustees' staffs prodded the actuaries to provide them with suitable forecasts in closed-door meetings provoked an uncharacteristically public burst of temper from
Steve Goss at the 2001 New York symposium. "David, you've
never been in the room," Goss exclaimed. "It's not true!"

Actuarial journals that had accepted Langer's submissions
for years suddenly closed their pages to him. Ex-commissioners
and other luminaries of the Social Security bureaucracy emerged
from obscurity to testify to the rigorous integrity of the actuarial
staff (although they conveniently glossed over the partisan character of the board of trustees). The furor grew strong enough to
obscure the value of his fundamental findings about the projections' inaccuracies.

Yet there's hardly any question that the 75-year forecasts do
afford the trustees considerable scope for subjectivity, if not outright manipulation. This has been the case since 1972, when benefits started to be indexed automatically to wage growth and

inflation. "Before that, there wasn't much political pressure," observes former chief actuary Haeworth Robertson, "mostly because there wasn't much opportunity for it."

As long as benefits were fixed, the actuaries had little reason even to speculate on future economic growth, wage trends, or inflation. Instead, every couple of years Congress would examine recent developments in economic growth and inflation, calculate how much money was flowing in from the payroll tax and how much purchasing power retirees had lost, and raise benefits accordingly.

Indexation forced the actuaries to look ahead as well as back. Henceforth, economic conditions, rather than congressional action, would govern the system's fiscal balance. The pressure was compounded by President Lyndon B. Johnson's so-called unification of the federal budget, by which Social Security's cash flow was no longer treated as distinct from all other federal accounts. The actuarial judgments affecting estimates of Social Security's surplus or deficit suddenly acquired political significance—they would play an important role in determining whether a president could claim to have balanced the entire federal budget.

Indeed, Robertson recalls facing political pressure from the Carter administration in 1977 over just such an issue. As chief actuary he had prepared a set of projections that were markedly more pessimistic than the previous year's. This didn't suit the White House, which was hoping to use a positive Social Security forecast to support its claim to have narrowed the deficit. Robertson says he was essentially overruled by the secretaries of Labor and the Treasury (both of whom were Social Security trustees), who refused to approve his estimates until they suggested a sunnier outlook.

Although it may be impossible to truly establish whether political pressure, no matter how subtle, colors the program's projections today, Langer certainly performed a public service by underscoring the fundamental haziness of the long-term forecasts. His work reminds us that the estimates coming out of the Social Security Administration are just that—educated guesses at best, not snapshots of an immutable future.

Critics like Langer don't question Social Security's general need for actuarial projections at all. It makes good sense for any enterprise whose fortunes are dependent on demographics and economics to try to deduce their likely direction from the historical record and current trends.

The tricky part is compiling a forecast that's neither too optimistic nor too pessimistic, for the opportunity for political mischief is great at either extreme. An optimistic projection for Social Security might encourage lawmakers to legislate richer benefits than can really be sustained, while an overly dire forecast can produce pressures for unwarranted cutbacks and tax increases. Hence the traditional three-pronged high-middle-low estimate.

The real question is why Social Security needs to look so far ahead into its future. The customary 75-year perspective, which is mandated by law, is based on two rationales. First, 75 years encompass roughly the length of an average American's life, so such a projection is likely to incorporate a cradle-to-grave picture of the system's impact on the average worker. Second, because legislated changes in Social Security can take decades to work their magic, a 75-year projection gives a reasonable, if generalized, picture of their effects.

A long-range crystal ball does have obvious limitations, however, chiefly that no one can possibly know what will happen even a day or two, much less three-quarters of a century, in the future. As a report for Congress's General Accounting Office observed in 2000, "Not many mortals voluntarily project demographic and economic assumptions for seventy-five years."

Even over the short term, cataclysmic events have a mischievous way of exposing the most cocksure prognosticators as abject fools. Who hasn't heard the story of the Yale economics professor, Irving Fisher, who declared on October 17, 1929, "Stocks have reached what looks like a permanently high plateau." Seven days later, the market crashed.

The only sure thing about the future is that it will never resemble our predictions. Consider only a few of the events and trends that would have eluded anyone trying to peer 75 years ahead into the American economy from a vantage point in 1930: the New Deal, World War II, the polio vaccine, the cold war, the space race, the fall of the Soviet Union, the oil shocks of the 1970s, the attacks of 9/11, and two wars in Iraq—not to mention the computer age, the rise of the Internet, and the growth of immigration, legal and illegal.

When one is juggling scores of variables with complex interrelationships, predictions that are even modestly off-kilter can produce huge misfires over time—in the same way that a mid-ocean navigational error of a few seconds of a degree can result, after a voyage of thousands of miles, in a vessel's landing on the wrong continent.

We can see how this effect operates by examining how the trustees' forecast of the growth of the trust fund has worked out in real time. This is the sort of error that occurs regularly in the Social Security forecasts.

In 1995, the trustees' intermediate estimate stated that the trust fund would be worth $781.28 billion at the end of 1999, adjusted for inflation. The best-case scenario projected an inflation-adjusted trust fund balance of $875.9 billion.

What actually happened? The year-end balance in 1999 turned out to be $896.1 billion. Over a mere four years, in other words, the trustees' intermediate projection—the one presumed to be the most accurate—missed the mark by almost $115 billion, an error of nearly 13 percent. But the best-case scenario was right on the money, with an error of less than 1 percent. (The worst-case scenario really was the worst; it underestimated the balance by 28 percent.)

The errors widened with time. The 1995 trustees' report's intermediate projection showed the trust fund reaching an inflation-adjusted $1.1 trillion in 2003, eight years hence. The best case pegged it at $1.44 trillion. The right number was $1.53 trillion, which put the intermediate estimate off by $430 billion, or 28 percent—more than a year's worth of paid benefits. The supposedly overoptimistic best-case scenario was off by less than 6 percent.

These are not rare or one-time miscalculations. David Langer's studies demonstrate that the intermediate forecast has consistently underestimated the trust fund assets by a wide margin for more than a decade. He reached this conclusion by checking each year's projection of the 2002 trust fund balance, starting with the trustees' 1992 report, against the actual balance at the end of 2002. Between 1992 and 1996, the intermediate projection was low every year by an average margin of more than 20 percent. The low-cost forecast, however, was almost always within 7 percent. (After 1997, all three projections began to converge toward the accurate number, which is what one would expect as the distance to 2002 shrank.)

Langer contends that the main cause of these inaccuracies is the trustees' persistent pessimism about U.S. gross domestic product, a proxy for overall economic growth. The GDP projection is central to the estimation of Social Security's solvency because it influences four other major factors in the actuarial model—average wages, growth in total employment, unemployment, and wage growth in excess of inflation.

The actuaries and trustees have underestimated correct GDP over the last 25 years by what Langer calculates to be a mean shortfall of more than 37 percent. In doing so, they appear to have resolutely ignored the historical record. Although the trustees acknowledged in their 2003 report that average real GDP growth (that is, growth in excess of inflation) over the 40 years from 1961 to 2001 had been 3.4 percent, they projected that the annual growth would fall to 1.8 percent through 2080—a rate that has not been consistently seen in the United States since the Great Depression.

The trustees justified this forecast by arguing that the passing of the baby boom would produce a sharp decline in labor force growth. But many economists consider that an extremely myopic viewpoint. As one recent Brookings Institution study observed, history suggests that such declines in the labor supply are often compensated for by improvements in productivity, birth rates, and immigration—all of which the trustees were predicting to remain low. Even though immigration had been growing at an average rate of 3.75 percent a year since 1970, the Brookings study pointed out, the trustees "somewhat incredibly . . . assume not just zero growth in the future, but an absolute decline from 1.4 million total immigrants in 2002 to a steady state after 2020 of 900,000 new immigrants a year."—The Brookings researchers flatly declared that projection to be "without any basis."

Such a divergence of opinion over economic growth plainly has tremendous implications for Social Security reform. If the trustees continue to be as off-base about economic growth as they have been in recent years, their forecasts will keep fueling fears that the program is lurching toward insolvency, lending support to those who favor its radical restructuring. But if economic growth continues to run well ahead of the projections, those fears will prove to be unfounded.

All of this underscores the folly of making dramatic, even historic, changes in Social Security based largely on long-term forecasts that may be no more reliable than carnival fortune-telling. And that is why the trustees' recent decision to publish a forecast of even more dubious reliability—a projection not merely to 75 years, but to infinity—seems so curious.

There are arguably good reasons for Social Security to speculate on its condition beyond a finite period. An open-ended projection helps policy makers appraise reform proposals that might have fiscal effects beyond the conventional 75-year horizon (including privatization schemes). But for most of us living today, the infinite projection has as much relevance as a cosmologist's speculation on the ultimate fate of the universe.

In unsophisticated hands, an infinite projection is as dangerous as a beaker of plutonium, because it so vastly magnifies the uncertainty already present in the 75-year projection. It's even hard to define: What exactly does it mean to project the fiscal condition of Social Security on an infinite time line?

As it happens, many in the actuarial community reacted with dismay to the trustees' decision to publish the new projection in their annual reports. One prominent critic was Eric J. Klieber, a Cleveland actuary who is chairman of the social insurance committee of the American Academy of Actuaries. His chief concern wasn't that the projection was useless to professionals, but that it was useless to laymen. He worried that the enormous dollar figures produced by the infinite projection, stripped of their technical context, would necessarily strike people as dramatic, impressive, even terrifying. He was particularly concerned about the trustees' calculation of Social Security's long-term deficit, or the imbalance of liabilities over assets that reflects the legacy debt.

Thanks to the magic of imputed interest, that deficit, which dates back to the benefits paid to the first generations of recipients, has continued to grow over the years. In 2005, the trustees calculated the present value of the deficit over the next 75 years—that is, the sum that would be needed in the present day to eliminate the shortfall over that period—as $4 trillion. That number seemed plenty big, but if one viewed it more sensibly as a ratio of the amount of money that would flow into Social Security over the same 75-year span, it lost much of its shock power. It came to only 1.92 percent of covered payroll, meaning that a rise in the payroll tax rate from 12.4 percent to 14.32 percent would cover all the red ink.

As Klieber foresaw, the infinite projection seemed to inflate the deficit to monstrous proportions—to $10.4 trillion. Although that larger figure still only amounted to 3.5 percent of covered payroll and 1.2 percent of gross domestic product through the infinite projection, the dollar amount carried all the punch of a thunderbolt. That effect alone made Klieber suspect that the infinite projection was more than an innocent actuarial device. He concluded that the trustees had taken a baldly political step, publishing the infinite projection "primarily as a scare tactic."

"I was concerned that it's such a very large number," he explained later on. "I was afraid people would see it and say, 'No one could possibly pay that.'"

Accordingly, as chairman of the actuaries' social insurance

committee he drafted a sharply worded letter to the trustees in December 2003, stating that the infinite projection results would "provide little if any useful information about [Social Security's] long-range finances and indeed are likely to mislead anyone lacking technical expertise." Their publication could only interfere with the "meaningful and balanced" picture that the trustees were sworn to provide to the public, he wrote, adding that in the charged political environment of the times, "speculative measures should be avoided."

Klieber pointed out another built-in danger of the infinite projection—for technical reasons, it would show an increase in the actuarial deficit each year, even if Social Security's fiscal condition held steady. This would inevitably foster more public alarm. "The public, seeing annual large increases in unfunded obligations, is likely to be misled into believing that the program's financial situation is deteriorating." (Indeed, in the 2005 report, the trustees revised their estimate from $10.4 trillion to $11.1 trillion, adding an imaginary $700 billion to the long-term deficit even though the system's fiscal situation hadn't deteriorated significantly.)

The trustees ignored Klieber's warning, but his fears came true. Almost from the moment the infinite projection was first published in 2003, the privatization lobby turned the figure into holy writ. Stripped of the abstruse technicalities of actuarial science, the enormous number could be exploited to make the cost of inaction seem dire indeed. In one display of moebius-strip logic, White House press secretary Scott McClellan dismissed as paltry the $2 trillion estimate of the cost of transitioning to private accounts. The $2 trillion, he said, would be "a savings, because the cost [of doing nothing] is $10 trillion . . . and this will actually be a savings from that cost of doing nothing."

President Bush wasted no opportunity to drill the big number into the public's head. His eyes wide with mock dismay, he repeated at his January 11 Mellon Auditorium dog-and-pony show: "This system of ours is going to be short the difference between obligations and money coming in, by about $11 trillion unless we act. That's trillion with a 'T.'"

No misrepresentation of the figure was too extreme to be aired by Social Security's enemies. Vice President Dick Cheney, speaking in Washington two days after the president's appearance, struggled to place the number in context, depicting it as "nearly twice the combined wages and salaries of every single working American last year"—thus underscoring how difficult it would be to solve an infinite funding problem in one short year, even for a can-do society like the United States of America. Sean Tufnell, an agent of the National Center for Policy Analysis, a front for such right-wing financiers as Richard Mellon Scaife and Joseph Coors and corporations such as ExxonMobil and Eli Lilly, wrote in the conservative *National Review* that bridging the gap could only be achieved by cutting benefits up to 30 percent, raising payroll taxes 50 percent, or borrowing $11 trillion—unless, that is, the government allowed workers to open private retirement accounts. ("An approach endorsed by President Bush," he added obligingly.)

In short order, the infinite forecast had become the privatization lobby's official symbol of the fiscal deterioration of Social Security. It represented the ultimate elevation of actuaries' murky foresight into received truth, the transformation of a speculative forecast pegged to the unimaginably distant future into a bogeyman for the present day.

Chapter Five

The Reagan Revolution Meets the Baby Boom

THERE PROBABLY has never been a demographic event better chronicled than the baby boom. The bulge in the fertility rate that occurred in the United States between 1946 and 1964 produced a generation that has been poked and prodded by psychologists, sociologists, and economists ever since its youngest members were in swaddling clothes. At every stage in their life cycle, they have been treated as monarchs of their world, dominant to an unprecedented degree in numbers, wealth, and political power. Their growth and maturity coincided exactly with that of postwar America. They were variously labeled the television generation, the Dr. Spock generation, the cold war generation, and the Vietnam generation; the heirs of the McCarthy era, the nuclear age, and the space age; and finally, the creators of the computer age.

The Social Security program has never been as well prepared to accommodate a new generation of beneficiaries as it will be for the baby boomers, who begin reaching full retirement age just after the start of the next decade. Nevertheless, the advent of the boomers has provoked extraordinary alarm about their effect on the system—warnings that they will bankrupt Social Security, impoverish their children and grandchildren, and leave the U.S. economy in ruins.

These are all misconceptions fostered by Social Security's enemies as a pretext for a radical reshaping of the program. But they originate in the peculiar financial circumstances that were impinging on the system just as the imminence of the boomer retirements was registering in the public's consciousness. That time was the early 1980s, when a genuine financial crisis really did threaten Social Security with collapse.

What made the Social Security crisis of 1983 so painful was that it arrived so unexpectedly on the heels of what experts would later call the system's "high-water mark." A mere ten years earlier, Social Security ranked as the undisputed star performer among U.S. government programs. It had fostered a sharp decline in poverty among the elderly, propped up the fortunes of millions of disabled persons and their dependents, and, after 1967, become the leading provider of medical care to senior citizens, too. Congress seized every opportunity it could to raise benefits or expand the program's reach with legislation that invariably proved crowd-pleasing. The neoclassical economist Paul Samuelson, who had become an improbable household name thanks to his regular column in *Newsweek,* proclaimed Social Security to be an emblem of economic potency.

"Everyone who reaches retirement age is given benefit privileges that far exceed anything he has paid in," he wrote in 1967. "How is it possible? It stems from the fact that the national product is growing at compound interest and can be expected to do so for as far ahead as the eye cannot see. . . . A growing nation is the greatest Ponzi game ever contrived."

What Samuelson's eye could not see was that storm clouds were already gathering. Several dangerous trends would come together during the next decade to knock Social Security off its pedestal.

The first was stagflation, an eerie combination of high inflation and low growth that afflicted the U.S. economy after the Arab oil shocks of 1973 and 1979. Real after-tax wages, which had been rising at more than 2.5 percent a year since the end of World War II, started falling in 1973. Women entered the workforce in greater numbers, partially to keep household budgets afloat. The birth rate plummeted.

Social Security itself had matured, and as the economist James Tobin observed, "growing up was a lot easier than adulthood." By the late 1970s, the program covered almost the entire U.S. workforce. Until then, it had always been able to improve its short-term fiscal profile by gathering in new groups of workers, for their payroll taxes would pump up the system's revenues for years before their retirements would begin to drain it. But the well was finally running dry. The only large group of uncovered workers remaining was state and local employees, who would resist inclusion to the bitter end; even today most of them are still exempt from mandatory enrollment in Social Security.

(The exclusion stems from Congress's reluctance in 1935 to impose a mandate on lower tiers of government; today their employees, most of whom obtain pension coverage through state pension plans, can be enrolled in Social Security's old-age and disability programs only through voluntary agreements between their states and the Social Security Administration. All state and local employees hired after April 1, 1986, however, are automatically enrolled in Medicare.)

The actions of successive Congresses to suck up any excess revenues by expanding coverage and benefits had kept the program's reserves low, as conservatives desired, but the slack had now been almost entirely taken up. Any further expansion of benefits would require a commensurate increase in the payroll tax rate.

Then, in 1972, came what is widely considered to be the worst blunder in the system's history—a botched attempt at inflation indexing that almost wrecked it for good.

Automatic inflation indexing was not a bad idea in principle. Prior to 1972, benefits had always been adjusted for inflation by Congress, which therefore had to periodically revisit the benefit formula and had grown weary of the chore. Social Security legislation always seemed to arise in even-numbered years—in other words, presidential or congressional election years—which created enormous tension between politicians' natural desire to please their constituents and their fear of busting the budget. When a proposal to shed Congress of the responsibility appeared in 1972, it was welcomed on Capitol Hill.

But 1972 was a presidential election year, and the roster of candidates for the Democratic nomination to oppose Richard Nixon's reelection included a clutch of prominent senators and congressmen. With Social Security benefits again on the table, they found themselves embroiled in an extended game of can-you-top-this, all jostling to advance the richest benefit package for retirees while Nixon administration officials stood by in bemusement. When the Social Security Administration placed a

5 percent across-the-board increase in benefits on the drawing board, its proposal was treated as a mere acorn from which a great oak might grow—within months it had morphed on Capitol Hill into a 20 percent increase, to be augmented by automatic annual cost-of-living raises. Anyone who murmured that the arrangement might be a bit overgenerous was promptly drowned out by a chorus of hosannas to the expanding U.S. economy. But the naysayers would turn out to be right.

For their part, veteran Social Security administrators could scarcely contain their delight. Robert Ball, who had helped manage the program almost since its infancy and was then nearing the end of his 11-year tenure as Social Security commissioner, said "a 20 percent benefit increase is really the difference between the program just limping along" and its having "a real impact."

Ball was especially pleased with automatic inflation indexing, which he had been pushing for years. The program's need to cadge retrospective inflation adjustments out of Congress always left recipients slightly behind the price curve. With an annual adjustment built in, the system finally seemed inflation-proof, Ball's long-desired goal. Nor did there seem to be much risk that benefits would outrun revenues. Revenues from the payroll tax increased along with wage growth, and benefits rose along with price gains, so the system's income would always rise more than its outflow. As Tobin observed, the rationale was that "wages grow faster than prices; anyway, they always had."

The 1970s would be the graveyard of such received economic wisdom. With the economy staggered by the OPEC oil embargoes and a collapse in labor productivity, the traditional formula was turned upside down. Price rises not only outran wage gains, they did so at a horrendous clip. While Social Security administrators looked on helplessly, the automatic inflation adjustments began to pump up benefits just at the moment when payroll tax revenues, linked as they were to wage growth, ceased to keep up.

There was one more miscalculation: The indexing formula embedded in the 1972 law included a technical error that over-compensated for inflation by awarding recipients credit for larger price increases than actually occurred. The mistake could not have come at a worse time, for a near-record bout of inflation was about to strike the country. It would take five years for Congress to get around to fixing the error, by which point it had blown a huge hole in Social Security's budget.

Even with the benefit of hindsight, historians today don't blame the economic soothsayers of the time for failing to predict the inflation surge of the mid-1970s, driven as it was by unexpected geopolitical developments. But the failure was on a major scale. As one study of the period notes, no forecast "had ever been so far off the mark in the history of Social Security." The system's actuaries had projected a rise in the consumer price index of 14.53 percent for 1972–1976; the real figure was 40.6 percent. The prediction for real wage growth (that is, over and above inflation) had been 11.77 percent for the same period; the real figure was 1 percent. The disparities sent the program on an accelerating downhill slide: The trustees' 1975 annual report warned that without an infusion of new revenues the system's reserve fund would be out of money by 1980.

The nation's leaders seemed at their wit's end. President Gerald Ford, who had succeeded the departed Richard Nixon, addressed the inflation challenge by asking Americans to wear lapel buttons reading WIN, for "Whip Inflation Now." Jimmy Carter, who followed him into the White House, decried the nationwide "crisis of confidence" in a televised address that became known as the "malaise" speech (although he never used that word himself).

In 1977, Carter introduced legislation to correct the indexing error of 1972 and restore a positive balance to the reserves, thus becoming the first president ever to propose a cut in Social Security benefits. His solution, however, still left the system hobbled. The reform ratcheted benefits for new retirees back from the 1972 level, but it left the higher formula in place for people who had already retired. This would help fuel criticism that Social Security was somehow a means for the elderly to cheat younger generations of the fruits of their labors. Although only those who retired from 1972 to 1977 reaped the gains of the flawed formula, the fiasco sowed a kernel of doubt in the system that its enemies would nurture into full-blown distrust.

The stage was set for the Reagan revolution.

Like other Americans whose formative years were darkened by the Great Depression, Ronald Reagan had always seemed constitutionally sympathetic to Social Security's broad goals—sympathetic, at least, to the principle of providing sustenance to the needy elderly. But as his politics morphed from the Democratic liberalism he espoused in the 1940s into the doctrinaire GOP conservatism of his California governorship and presidential career, his position on the program also shifted. By 1960, Reagan had become openly critical of the system's size and, as was typical for a conservative Republican, of its funding scheme.

He was convinced, he wrote later, "that Americans had been deceived regarding the security of their money that was deducted from their paychecks to pay for Social Security benefits . . . it had become a compulsory tax producing revenues Congress could—and did—use for any purpose it wanted."

On the presidential stump, Reagan often lumped Social Security advisers with the traditional welfare programs he casually vilified as part of his natural campaign *shtick*—a habit that his own advisers feared could become something of an electoral Achilles' heel as long as Social Security, then approaching its golden anniversary, was still politically sacrosanct. Reagan's expressed opinion of all such so-called entitlement programs came filtered through his customary scrim of cautionary anecdotes. One chestnut about a putative Chicago welfare queen who carried enough fraudulent Social Security cards to finance a tax-free $150,000 lifestyle became such a cherished part of his repertoire that his aides, sensing its approach by the rhythms of his speech, would nudge each other in shared tedium.

Years later, in his memoirs, he was still rehashing the same theme. Democratic accusations that "we were plotting to throw senior citizens to the wolves" had forced him to "withdraw a plan to cut billions of dollars in waste and fraud from the Social Security system," he groused, noting that "among other abuses, we'd discovered monthly Social Security checks were being sent to eighty-five hundred people who'd been dead an average of eighty-one months." He seemed oblivious to the fact that, in a system that was serving 31 million beneficiaries when he took office in 1981, the error rate represented by this spectacular find came to less than three-hundredths of one percent, a standard of precision that probably matched that of the moon program.

With Barry Goldwater's campaign stumbles on Social Security reform still fresh in Republican memories 20 years after the fact, Reagan's own campaign handlers went to great lengths to distance the candidate from any concrete proposal to cut benefits or raise payroll taxes. They would have been content if the issue remained quiescent for his entire presidency. Before his first term was over, however, two obstacles prevented a clean getaway. One was the maneuvering of David Stockman, a dyed-in-the-wool Reagan revolutionary who had been appointed director of the White House office of management and budget. The second was the appearance of an authentic Social Security financial crunch.

Despite having grown up as the grandson of a preacher and served two terms as a congressman from Michigan, Stockman had arrived at the White House with a rock-hard soul and a political tin ear. Infused with a radical fervor for the budget slashing and tax cutting that, accepting Reagan's campaign rhetoric as gospel, he understood to be official administration policy, Stockman had trained his gunsights from the start on Social Security. The program was "the very inner fortress of the American welfare state," he wrote later, "a capricious hybrid of out-and-out welfare benefits and earned pension annuities, which were hopelessly tangled together and disguised under the fig leaf of social insurance."

Stockman regarded Social Security as a relic not merely of the New Deal but of LBJ's antipoverty Great Society. In his eyes, whatever virtues had ever existed in its mission to assist the poor had become submerged beneath an accretion of entitlements for the comfortable. Social Security was "closet socialism" and a "giant Ponzi scheme." Its reserves posed such a temptation to politicians wishing to bribe constituents with unearned benefits that it cursed them with "something close to original sin."

And that was just the old-age pension program. Stockman was just as contemptuous of the disability program, which he regarded as lax in its eligibility standards and profligate in its largesse. He was offended that the checks mailed to two disabled workers who had made identical contributions to the system could differ markedly, merely because one was supporting a spouse and dependents and the other was single and childless.

No bureaucrat who viewed disability protection largely as "a powerful temptation to the shiftless" or deride the system's redistributive properties as "arbitrary and costly," as Stockman did, would ever be swayed by arguments based on the principles of social insurance, such as those that had accompanied the birth of Social Security in the 1930s and its expansion in the 1950s and 1960s. Indeed, he wasn't.

His downfall, however, wasn't caused by his blindness to Social Security's principles, but by his insensitivity to its politics. Although he certainly understood that it was a program "on which one-seventh of the nation's populace depended for its well-being," he didn't seem to realize that those people, the people who cared for them, and the members of Congress who represented them comprised a vast and determined interest group.

That's not to say that Stockman was entirely unaware that any proposal to cut benefits would meet with a Capitol Hill recoil. In early 1981, as he was drafting a budget that would cut federal spending by $130 billion, he deliberately concealed his intention to extract $44 billion of the total from Social Security behind a catch-all item formally labeled "future savings to be identified." This nebulous provision would soon acquire an uncomplimentary moniker, "the magic asterisk." As Stockman described it later, the magic asterisk encompassed "the true heavy lifting, politically speaking, of the Reagan fiscal revolution." It was an arrow aimed directly at "the big middle-class entitlement programs," of which he considered Social Security to be the 600-

pound gorilla. But he intended to keep the arrow sheathed until the very last moment.

In the course of his determined campaign to single-handedly dismantle Social Security, Stockman waved away several more politically palatable ideas from Capitol Hill. Aware that the ill-advised 1970s reforms and the worsening economic climate had produced a fiscal crisis for the program, astute lawmakers in both parties had proposed such reforms as gradually raising the normal retirement age from 65 to 68 and extending coverage to state and local government workers.

Privately, Stockman dismissed these as "paltry" distractions. His approach was heavy-duty. He intended to dramatically tighten the eligibility rules for disability, eliminate payments to some dependents, and tighten the cap on the total of certain benefits that could be paid to any one family.

But the centerpiece of his program was a dramatic increase in the early-retirement penalty, imposed on those who retired between the ages of 62 and 65, raising it from 20 percent to 45 percent of the normal retirement stipend. What's more, Stockman scheduled the change to go into effect almost immediately. To say that the cut, from an average $469 a month to $310, would come as an unwelcome surprise to thousands of workers who already had set their retirement dates and calculated their benefits under the old rules, is a massive understatement. It would be a political bombshell.

Stockman buried his explosive nugget in a background paper deliberately couched, as he later gloated, in "perfectly incomprehensible Social Security Administration format and jargon which obscured almost everything," and furnished it with "a cover memo which explained almost nothing." He sent the impenetrable package to the White House on a Friday so the president's top aides would have only two weekend days to digest it (if they could) before presenting it to the president. The following Monday morning, Stockman ambled over to the executive mansion for an Oval Office meeting that ranks as one of the great comic opera moments of the Reagan presidency.

"Only sixty minutes had been allotted for that meeting on May 11 with the president—not much time for him to review a plan which in both philosophy and detail reversed forty-five years of Social Security history," he wrote five years later, still exuding undisguised glee at his own cunning. Reagan, not yet fully recovered from John Hinkley's assassination attempt a few weeks earlier, listened to Stockman's presentation with "his eyes glazed by technical detail," one participant recalled. Evidently, the president grasped only a few of his budget director's most elementary talking points. These included Stockman's observation that an early-retirement option had not been part of the original Social Security plan, and that the changes he was proposing would place the entire program on a sound fiscal footing for the first time in years. "You'll be the first president in history to honestly and permanently fix Social Security," one of Stockman's deputies told Reagan, appealing cannily to his amour propre. "No one else has had the courage to do it." Before the president's alarmed political aides could intervene, Reagan approved the entire proposal on the spot.

Within 48 hours, the early-retirement provision ignited a quintessential Washington firestorm. Stockman later pleaded that he "just hadn't thought through the impact of making it effective immediately," but he had set himself up as the fall guy. The reform package got ruthlessly hammered on the floor of Congress and in the national press. Tip O'Neill of Massachusetts, the colorful Speaker of the House of Representatives, accused the Republicans of trying "to balance the budget on the backs of the elderly," coining a sound bite that would do yeoman work for the defenders of Social Security for the next 20 years. A little more than a week after the meeting in the Oval Office, Stockman's package was pronounced dead, with a unanimous 96-0 vote against it in the U.S. Senate serving as the eulogy.

Years later, the economist William A. Niskanen, a member of Reagan's Council of Economic Advisers and subsequently chairman of the right-wing Cato Institute, would describe the fiasco in words that echoed Alf Landon's rueful postmortem of his own attack on Social Security. Niskanen called the package "the major domestic policy mistake of the Reagan administration—an extraordinary political misjudgment." Reagan biographer Lou Cannon observed that the debacle's impact resounded far beyond Social Security itself; it marked the end of "any major assault against the basic premises of the federal budget" by Reagan, who was less than a year into his first term. Thanks in large part to the aborted attack, 26 Republican congressmen would lose their seats in the 1982 midterm elections.

By then the administration had placed Social Security policy under strict quarantine. In late 1981, the White House punted the issue of the program's financial status into the lap of a presidential panel labeled the National Commission on Social Security Reform. As Stockman later described this action, with a characteristic snarl from the wilderness to which he had been consigned, the White House "fobbed off Social Security to a bipartisan study commission whose instructions were to take a year to think about it."

But before its work was done, the commission that had been born so inauspiciously would successfully extricate the system from the worst financial emergency in its history.

At first, official Washington took an ambivalent attitude toward the 15-member commission. No one expected much from the panel, given its improbable mandate to relieve the program's financial strain without sullying the political fortunes of either Republicans or Democrats. As though hoping to usher it swiftly offstage, Reagan gave the commission a tight deadline— December 31, 1982—to prepare a plan of reform. Representative Barber Conable, a respected Republican from upstate New York, publicly dismissed the very idea of a commission as a "cop-out"—and he had been appointed one of its *members*. Robert Ball, the former Social Security commissioner who represented House Speaker O'Neill on the panel, told a reporter he considered it merely a device to defer discussion of Social Security reform until the 1982 midterm elections were safely past.

On the other hand, the prominence of the appointees and their breadth of experience ensured that any recommendations they did propose would be well received in the capital. The panel consisted of seven Republicans and six Democrats, with five members appointed by the president and ten jointly by the four congressional party leaders. The business community was represented by the chairman of Prudential Insurance and the president of the National Association of Manufacturers; organized labor, by Lane Kirkland, the president of the AFL-CIO. The presence of four sitting U.S. senators and five current or former members of Congress gave the body peerless political credibility. The chairman was Alan Greenspan, a former chairman of the Council of Economic Advisers under President Ford, who was running his own economic consulting firm during a sort of entr'acte before returning to government in 1987 as chairman of the Federal Reserve Board.

In retrospect, the Greenspan commission represents something of a high-water mark for presidential advisory panels on Social Security. It was bipartisan, unburdened by a preconceived agenda, and receptive to a wide range of solutions to the mounting Social Security deficit. In completing its labors more than a year later, it issued a ringing endorsement of the structure and principles of the Social Security system as they had existed since 1935—the last such endorsement of its kind by any presidential advisory body.

For all that, the commissioners dithered for several months after their swearing-in. Installed in a cramped townhouse down the street from the White House and across from the Executive Office Building, they passed excruciating hours being force-fed arid presentations by Social Security bureaucrats about the system's procedures and economics. Finally, Ball, who was serving as an unofficial chief of staff for the panel's Democratic minority, put an end to the lecture series so the group could focus on the issues at hand.

Those issues were becoming more urgent by the moment. The system's finances were on the brink of collapse. Soon after taking office, the commission received word from the Social Security Administration that its reserve ratio at the start of 1983 would be only 10 percent of the coming year's benefits, a shockingly low number, and that it would be in the red before the year was out. The trustees let it be known that benefit checks for July 1983 would not be mailed out unless a repair was in place before then. Considering that the program had never missed a monthly payment, this was a deadline that could not be broken without causing a public uproar, with severe consequences for politicians in both parties.

Even the system's best-case projection showed the trust fund for the old-age program running out of money no later than 1984. The short-term deficit of $150 billion to $200 billion projected through 1989 was only the most pressing aspect of the crisis. A long-term deficit of $1.6 trillion loomed for the 75-year forecast period beyond that.

Although the range of the commission's possible solutions was theoretically infinite, early in its deliberations it removed certain ideas from the table. One was a proposal to replace Social Security with a system of private savings accounts. The concept was presented to the panel by Michael J. Boskin, a conservative economist from Stanford University who would later become chairman of the Council of Economic Advisers for President George H. W. Bush. Even the most conservative members of the commission recognized that Boskin's plan would be too extreme a departure from the traditions of Social Security. They let him know that if an innovative policy such as privatization were to be considered at all, that would be the job of some other commission, not theirs.

Still, at the beginning of December 1982, despite the looming year-end deadline and the system's encroaching fiscal moment of truth, the commission was on the verge of failure. Ball and the Democrats had proposed solving the short-term deficit largely by moving a scheduled 1990 payroll tax increase up by six years, to 1984. They adamantly rejected any cuts in benefits, beyond minor adjustments. The Republicans took the opposite position, objecting to the tax increase and insisting on sizable program reductions. The White House steered clear of the whole subject, contributing nothing to the discussion except a signal that it would reject any tax increase. The commission's regular monthly meeting in December broke up in stalemate after 15 minutes. In desperation, Greenspan asked Reagan to extend the panel's brief for 30 days into the new year; the president granted him 15.

As often happens in Washington, however, there were stirrings behind the scenes. The Reagan administration couldn't afford to be entirely disinterested in the commission's success or failure; if it failed, the Social Security mess would only end up back in the White House's lap.

Accordingly, one day in mid-December a White House aide named Richard Darman phoned Ball and invited him to meet for a conversation that would have to remain absolutely confidential. (Ball's memo for his own files referred to the meeting as "Meeting which never took place on December 17, 1982.") Darman warned Ball that powerful figures in the administration were poised to take advantage of a commission failure. Martin Feldstein, a free-market economist whose star was rising inside the White House, was goading the president to place major cuts in Social Security before Congress. Reagan himself had been heard to ponder whether to "go to the people" with a campaign to phase out the program entirely.

Eyeball to eyeball with such a threat, Ball blinked. He drafted a rescue plan that would yield more than $75 billion in savings by delaying a scheduled cost-of-living increase by six months and taxing some benefits paid to wealthy retirees. Meanwhile, the commission's Republican dean, Senator Robert Dole—himself alert to the consequences of failure—hinted quietly that the Republican commissioners might accede to a tax increase if it were suitably coupled with a few benefit changes.

These ideas became the kernel of a solution worked out in secret by a rump committee made up of five commission members and a clutch of White House advisers, including, of all people, David Stockman. On January 15, right at the wire, they reached an agreement.

The 1983 reform package would later be held up as a model of bipartisan concord. It would also stand as Social Security's last unambiguous victory over its ideological enemies: in its very first formal recommendation, the commission stated that Congress "should not alter the fundamental structure of the Social Security program or undermine its fundamental principles." The commission's final report noted specifically that the panel had considered, but rejected, proposals to make the program voluntary, to turn it into a defined-contribution plan via private accounts, and to re-fashion it as a welfare program limited to the indigent.

The commission carefully balanced its solution to the pending fiscal crisis between benefit cuts and tax increases. A few new concepts appeared, including improved monthly benefits for those who retired later than the normal retirement age, which was then 65. For the first time, all newly hired federal employees were subject to mandatory enrollment in Social Security. (State and local government workers, however, retained their exemption.) Benefits for early retirees were scaled back, but only gradually over the period from 1990 to 1999, a timetable that minimized the sort of backlash that had greeted Stockman's plan.

Among the package's most important features was that it asked the baby boomers to fund their own retirements in advance. "Between 1990 and 2010," one analysis noted, "the huge baby boom generation would be in its peak earning years, and the numbers of new retirees would be below normal, as the relatively few people born during the Great Depression and World War II entered beneficiary status."

The commission saw this as a window of opportunity. The payroll tax increase that kicked in during those years would produce enough revenue to fund current benefits *and* produce a handsome surplus, which would be banked against the baby boomer tide by parking the money in government bonds. The commission not only anticipated the decline in the ratio of workers to retirees that would appear with the baby-boomer retirements—the scary-sounding statistic trotted out so often today as a symbol of Social Security's inherent instability—but fully factored it into the tax schedule. The way the fiscal balancing act was to work, the surplus taxes would build the trust fund to a peak of more than $20 trillion in 2045. From then on, the fund would be drawn down year by year, like a water tank during a drought, to cover the shortfall between current taxes and the payouts to baby-boomer retirees. When it reached its projected exhaustion in 2063, the youngest baby boomer would be 99 years old. No one could see a flaw in the system.

Congress made one significant change in the commission's proposal, enacting a gradual increase in the normal retirement age from 65 to 67 by 2027, a date that seemed comfortably remote.

In terms of legislative time, the Social Security package sped through Congress, reaching Reagan's desk before April 20. The president's doubts about Social Security and his aides' hostility to its principles were forgotten in the glow of a successful bailout. Reagan, who supposedly had been at work a few weeks earlier on a plan to abolish the whole system, now preened in the role of its savior. At the signing ceremony he invoked FDR, citing what he called Roosevelt's commitment that "Social Security must always provide a secure and stable base so that older Americans may live in dignity."

———

"My fellow Americans," he added, "I think we've gotten a very great deal."

Social Security, once again the darling of public opinion, was back on its feet. The threat from the Reagan revolution, such as it was, had receded. The national commitment to its basic structure as a social insurance program had been renewed, and a general optimism about the near-term economy spilled over into optimism about the system's fiscal balance.

The glow would scarcely last a decade. And once it faded, the system's enemies, having prepared the terrain, would be ready to attack.

Chapter Six

The Myth of the Mythical Trust Fund

F OR AN ILLUSTRATION of how big lies get spread through tiny kernels of misinformation, consider the short feature broadcast by PBS's *NewsHour with Jim Lehrer* in October 2004, a few days before the show's host was to moderate the first presidential debate between President Bush and Senator John Kerry.

To illuminate the fiscal challenge facing Social Security, the program's reporter, Paul Solman, had gone off in search of the trust fund, that $1.5-trillion hoard that will supposedly guarantee the benefits promised retirees through 2041—the very fund that presidential candidate Al Gore had pledged to safeguard in a "lockbox" during his ill-starred 2000 campaign.

The hunt brought Solman to the red-brick headquarters of the Federal Bureau of Public Debt in Parkersburg, West Virginia.

"This is it?" he exclaimed, disbelievingly, standing before a file cabinet inside the building. "This is the lockbox we heard so much about?"

Scarcely suppressing his mirth, Solman pulled open a drawer and leafed through the contents, page after page, each attesting to $11 billion in obligations owed by the U.S. Treasury to the future beneficiaries of Social Security. "All we've been locking in the box are copies of IOU's that we, the people, owe to ourselves," he marveled aloud. "Another $11 billion . . . and another $11 billion. . . . So this is, like, $100 billion in this folder . . ."

The implication, as Solman drew it out in a series of subsequent interviews, was that the $1.5 trillion trust fund is a sham—that the money isn't piled away safely somewhere, against the moment when Social Security needs it to make good on its checks. Instead, it's just a bunch of IOUs, about as trustworthy as pledges made by a horseplayer to his bookie.

One might ask what exactly Solman expected to find at the end of his search for evidence of the sacred promise made by the Treasury of the United States to its own taxpayers. Gold bars sequestered in a basement corner beneath Fort Knox, like the ingots James Bond saved from destruction in *Goldfinger*? Towering mounds of cash? A diamond as big as the Ritz?

The assets that Solman did find and so casually denigrated as mere "IOUs" were just as real as those a bank customer keeps on deposit, evidenced as his or her property by a monthly statement received in the mail—just as real, indeed, as a dollar bill, which is itself a piece of paper representing a purely metaphorical promise by the U.S. government to deliver specie to the owner upon demand.

Solman is an award-winning reporter with solid credentials in business and economic journalism. In this case, however, he had become a carrier of the most insidious smear levied against

Social Security by its enemies—that the trust fund is nothing but a trillion-dollar bookkeeping exercise or, worse, a deliberate fraud.*

He told me later that he was trying to address "the nub of the debate" over the so-called lockbox: "Did the government salt away any money or not? Did it sequester the money? The answer is no."

As far as that answer goes, he is correct. The problem is that he asked the wrong question. For the "nub of the issue" is not whether the government has parked money belonging to Social Security in some dark corner, not to be touched until it's needed in another 40 or 50 years. The issue is where the money has come from, and how it has been spent.

The truth is that Social Security's reserve has been built up from assets belonging to millions of working taxpayers. It's money the government has collected in payroll taxes since 1983 over and above the system's current needs, on the representation that the surplus will eventually be spent to cover the cost spike caused by the retirement of baby boomers.

In practice, the money has amounted to a huge loan from the middle class and poor, who pay most of the payroll tax, to the wealthy, who pay the bulk of income taxes. The income tax rates of the rich have been kept low by four presidential administrations, which have raided the trust fund to pay for federal programs that should have been financed from the income tax levy. The question Solman should have asked was: Why shouldn't the wealthy be obligated to pay the loan back?

But he's not alone in redefining a $1.5-trillion loan from the working-class to the rich as an uncollectible IOU. Some of the

---

*Actually three trust funds, one each for the old age, disability, and Medicare programs. For the purposes of simplicity, we'll refer to "trust fund" in the singular, to denote the old-age and disability funds.

---

nation's most distinguished policy makers and pundits have done the same.

"I think the trust fund belongs well up there in American oxymorons," Peter G. Peterson, a wealthy former Commerce Secretary and president of the Federal Reserve Bank of New York, advised Solman when he returned from his West Virginian odyssey, "because it shouldn't be trusted, and it's not funded. What you've been doing is not stashing money away. You've been stashing IOU's away."

"The Social Security system has no trust fund. No lockbox," seconded *Washington Post* columnist Charles Krauthammer in February 2005. "When you pay your payroll tax every year, the money is not converted into gold bars and shipped to some desert island, ready for retrieval when you turn 65. A piece of paper gets deposited in a vault in West Virginia saying that the left hand of the government owes money to the right hand of the government."

Even luminaries who once held direct responsibility for the trust fund have participated in this charade. After she left the government and put out her shingle as a corporate consultant, former Social Security commissioner Dorcas R. Hardy called the trust fund "a shell game." Every U.S. Treasury bond issued to the Social Security system, she wrote, is "an IOU . . . backed by the full faith and credit of the federal government, *but not by anything else*" (my emphasis).

At a meeting of corporate leaders in 2001, then-treasury secretary Paul O'Neill risked provoking a global financial meltdown by declaring that "we have no assets in the trust fund. We have promises of the good faith and credit of the United States government that benefits will flow."

Not many people could have been listening closely to the man who was then serving as Social Security's managing trustee.

Otherwise, someone might have asked him to explain the meaning of pages 19 and 23 of the annual trustees' report to which he had signed his name a few weeks earlier, which certified the existence of assets of $1 trillion in U.S. government securities, including some $152 billion in new bonds purchased on his watch.

The literature of the Heritage Foundation, the Cato Institute, and other privatization promoters bristles with similar rhetoric. Sometimes the publishers unwittingly reveal their secret convictions about the U.S. government, as when Heritage contended in a 1999 pamphlet that the trust fund "contains no genuine assets, *only government bonds.*"

The securities these people denigrate as worthless aren't old certificates that have been collecting dust for a century, like Confederate dollars or tsarist bonds. They're bonds that Social Security has purchased from the Treasury over the last 20 years, precisely on the understanding that someday they'll be redeemed for cash. Despite all the supposed warning signs that it's buying worthless paper, the system *continues to buy them*—at a clip of roughly $150 billion a year.

The average person might think that only idiots or crooks would dump so much money into worthless securities. But the Social Security board of trustees includes three members of President Bush's cabinet (as of 2005, Treasury Secretary John Snow, Labor Secretary Elaine Chao, and Health and Human Services Secretary Mike Leavitt), along with the Social Security commissioner and two upstanding members of the public.

What's wrong with this picture?

On the surface, one would never think that it could be unwise to invest in U.S. Treasury securities. They're regarded around the globe as the safest investments anyone can own, largely because the U.S. government has never defaulted on a single obligation. They're the most glittering of all gilt-edged bonds, so secure that investors ranging from American citizens and major financial institutions to sovereign foreign governments clamor to own them despite their offering what are among the lowest interest payouts of any bonds anywhere.

To label the bonds owned by Social Security "merely IOUs" is to paint them as fundamentally different from the other $4 trillion in bonds owned by the federal government's other creditors.

All these securities, however, are backed by the identical pledge of the "full faith and credit" of the U.S. government. The phrase represents more than a conditional undertaking subject to the government's willingness to honor it. The U.S. government's full faith and credit has long been assumed to be good enough collateral to make those securities rock-solid without the backing of (in Dorcas Hardy's words) "anything else."

Today's global financial system is dependent on such promises. As Social Security experts Henry J. Aaron and Robert D. Reischauer pointed out in the 1990s, "neither Social Security nor private financial savers, including individuals and pension funds, hold 'real' assets in their accounts. Both hold IOUs—paper promises of some private or public entity to pay interest or dividends." Those assets are only as good as the issuer's commitment make good on them upon demand. In fact, millions of taxpayers who invested in the personal retirement accounts so enthusiastically promoted by the "privatization" lobby would probably be buyers of such U.S. government "IOUs" because of their perceived safety.

It's worth noting that the jaundiced view of the trust fund assets being aired today is relatively new. It certainly was not the view of the Greenspan commission in 1983.

The trust fund was an essential piece of the commission's strategy for keeping Social Security fiscally sound through the baby-boom retirement wave. The panel spent hours discussing how to build up the reserve and where to put the accumulating cash. In the end, they proposed a detailed set of rules governing how the fund should be invested, under what circumstances it could be spent or transferred among the system's programs, and even whether the surplus should be accounted for as part of the overall federal budget. Most of these technicalities aren't important to us as laymen, except that they underscore that the trust fund, in the view of these saviors of Social Security, was the very essence of a hard asset.

What lies behind this concerted effort to destroy confidence in the Social Security trust fund?

One motive is certainly strategic. It's hard to describe Social Security as careening toward a crisis as long as it owns $1.5 trillion in reserve assets. Belittling those assets as mythical, therefore, is a necessary first step in portraying the system as destitute. If the $1.5 trillion in the fund truly does not represent a claim on the federal government—if it's imaginary, as the privatization lobby would have it—then the system indeed might be "flat busted" by 2018, President Bush's choice for the day of reckoning.

That year, according to the trustees' intermediate-case projection, the cost of scheduled benefits will start to outrun revenues in payroll taxes; the system must begin to make up the shortfall by spending the interest payments it has recorded from its treasuries. Bereft of the interest, the system would be more than $60 billion in the hole in 2018, and the deficit would widen from there. So it's unsurprising that the privatizers argue that the system's claim for interest on its bond holdings is as much an evanescent dream as its claim on the bond principal. (Heritage has called the interest payments "demonstrably meaningless.")

The second reason for willing the bonds out of existence is that liquidating them to cover scheduled benefits in the future will require a large-scale redistribution of income from the wealthy to the middle class and poor starting approximately in 2021 and lasting through 2041 (according to the intermediate-case scenario) or 2053 (according to the nonpartisan Congressional Budget Office). As it happens, this redistribution is nothing more than a repayment of the subsidy that the affluent have been receiving from all other taxpayers since 1983. To understand this process more clearly, we need to step back in time and examine how the Social Security system came to acquire such a large holding of U.S. Treasury securities in the first place.

The roots of the trust fund's investment policy can be found, like so much else about the present-day system, in the debate over its creation in 1935.

As we have seen, one of the more contentious topics was how to finance Social Security over the long term. The drafting committee eventually settled on a compromise in which the program would eventually build up a reserve of about $47 billion from payroll tax revenues.

Conservatives were unnerved by the very size of the reserve fund. In 1935, many people found the idea of a $47-billion government hoard "too fantastic to comprehend." After all, the entire federal budget that year was only $6.3 billion.

Critics were leery of placing so much wealth in the hands of the federal government. Conservative legislators and businessmen had nightmares of a "federal government undertaking a social investing program that they philosophically abhorred." They feared that, by tapping a Social Security slush fund, the government in Washington would be able to extend its reach into new areas of policy and to interfere, through the sheer exercise of fiscal power, in matters traditionally left to the states. They were also afraid that the money would burn a hole in Congress's pocket— that legislators, anxious to please their demanding constituents, would spend the money in the reserve by approving profligate expansions in benefits and coverage.

One question that deeply concerned policy makers across the political spectrum was where to invest the money. Every option was unpalatable to someone. Limiting the reserve's investments to Treasury securities would mean, in effect, expanding the national debt to unimaginable size. The total outstanding federal debt at the time was $27 billion, and many in Congress were looking forward to paying it off after the Depression had run its course, not adding to it—and certainly not tripling it.

Allowing the fund to invest in private securities hardly seemed a better option. Few generations in modern American history could have been more viscerally aware of the riskiness of the capital markets. More than 85 percent of the stock market's value had been wiped out between the crash of 1929 and 1932, and the waves of ruin produced by the cataclysm were still washing over the countryside.

Even if the public were emotionally ready for renewed investments in stocks, the sums available for investment would place the government among the most potent investors in the country, powerful enough to make policy in the corporate boardroom. To some political leaders, government ownership of private enterprise on such a scale was out of the question. When Arthur Altmeyer, one of the system's founders, proposed to the conservative Republican senator Arthur Vandenberg that the system invest *only* in private securities, the lawmaker wryly turned away the suggestion. "That would be socialism," he said. He didn't seem to take the idea seriously.

Altmeyer, in fact, did harbor thoughts of investing in assets other than government bonds. He viewed the reserve as an instrument for extending Social Security's influence far beyond old-age assistance—investing in "social undertakings such as . . . low-cost housing, schools, hospitals," and even in manufacturing that "could be justified from the point of view of social welfare." As this suggests, the conservatives' nightmares about the reach of the federal government may well have been rooted in reality.

The conservatives won the first skirmishes of the battle. Over the next several decades they relentlessly fought against reserve fund growth, sometimes by legislating freezes or reductions in the payroll tax when the revenues exceeded what was needed for current benefits, and sometimes by allowing benefits and coverage to expand. A package of amendments in 1950 increased benefits by 80 percent and added 10 million new workers to the rolls, including domestic help, farmworkers, and the self-employed; proposals to add disability benefits and to improve survivor and spousal stipends followed, all winning conservative support partially because they soaked up spare cash. With the reserve reduced to well below the $47 billion that FDR's Treasury secretary, Henry Morgenthau, had considered prudent, Social Security eventually evolved into the pure pay-as-you-go system that conservatives had preferred all along.

Keeping a lid on the reserve, however, meant that the payroll tax became much more sensitive to the program's demands. A series of tax increases to keep Social Security solvent began in the 1950s and 1960s. Nevertheless, the program entered what might be termed its "era of good feeling." The old debates over funding seemingly had been laid to rest. Even the tax hikes failed to elicit much objection from the generations then paying in and anticipating retirement, for "Social Security was widely perceived as being an extremely good deal."

But it wouldn't be long before the ancient disagreements recurred. What set the stage were the economic shocks that rattled the country in the 1970s—two sudden increases in oil prices, which led to high inflation concurrent with slow economic growth (the dreaded "stagflation"). Amendments enacted in 1977 under President Jimmy Carter changed benefit formulas, sharply raised the payroll tax, and made other changes designed to adapt the system to a dramatically altered economic environment. (In the spirit of the age, the law made a few socially oriented improvements, too, including making it gender-neutral by replacing all references to "wives" and "women" with "spouse" and "participant." As one commentator observed later, "The law no longer made any presumption that the secondary earner was female.")

But the changes were insufficient. When conditions in the 1980s forced the Reagan administration to revisit the system's financing, one of the key elements in the new fix was a return to the concept of advance funding that had been part of the original act in 1935. The reserve was back, in the guise of the Social Security trust fund. And so were all the old questions about how and where to invest the money. One thing would be different, however. The system was about to accumulate vastly more capital than Henry Morgenthau or Arthur Vandenberg had envisioned in their wildest dreams.

The changes in benefits and tax rates enacted by Congress on the Greenspan commission's recommendations were partially designed to prepare Social Security for the coming wave of retiring baby boomers. Under the new schedule of tax rates, the combined old-age and disability trust fund, which had peaked at $1.1 billion in 1950 and had been steadily drawn down since then, was projected to reach $52 billion by the end of 1986—and to keep growing.

As long as federal law limited the fund to investing in Treasury securities, its opportunity cost of avoiding better-paying investments like corporate equities—that is, the forgone income that more aggressive investments might yield—rose exponentially. When the fund totaled $52 billion, a 4 percentage-point difference in yield between a Treasury bond and a diversified portfolio of stocks would amount to more than $2 billion a year; but when the fund reached $1 trillion, as it did in 2001, the opportunity cost had ballooned to $40 billion, or enough to pay one month's benefit to every Social Security recipient. The potential gains made a Social Security investment in the stock market look very inviting. The market still might be risky, but any fund the program might sponsor presumably would be large enough to be effectively diversified.

A sizable federal investment in corporate securities, however, still raised touchy economic, political, and philosophical issues. The potential for conflicts of interest was inescapable. The government might turn out to be a major holder of shares in a corporation it was prosecuting for criminal activity or suing as a polluter. It might have a financial interest in a merger that violated the national interest in terms of antitrust policy. It might stand to profit financially from a bid by foreign investors for a company that national security dictated should remain in American hands. Controversies over public investments in companies involved in apartheid-era South Africa demonstrated that the government might conceivably end up on one side of an international issue as a member of the community of nations, and on the other side as a shareholder.

The tobacco industry placed the potential for messy conflicts in particularly sharp relief. As Sylvester Schieber and John R. Shoven observed, in his 1999 State of the Union address, President Bill Clinton simultaneously threatened to sue the tobacco industry over its impact on public health and proposed to allow the Social Security Administration to invest broadly in all equities, tobacco not excepted.

Many people doubted Congress's ability to resist using the trust fund's investment clout as a political or social tool. Counterarguments pointing to the ability of the federal Thrift Savings Plan, whose four index funds invest the retirement contributions of millions of federal employees, to resist political pressure were not entirely convincing. With roughly $100 billion in assets, the TSP is a pipsqueak compared to the Social Security trust fund. Moreover it has clear-cut fiduciary responsibilities to its members that would be violated if it pursued any so-called social investment policy. The Social Security trust fund, whose contributions come from mandatory taxes, wouldn't have the same relationship to its enrollees.

In any case, the behavior of several state pension funds belied the example of the TSP. Starting in the 1980s and 1990s, the California Public Employee Retirement System and the New York State Teachers Retirement Fund—to name two of the largest institutional investment funds in the country—emerged as leaders in campaigns to divest shares in companies involved in tobacco and South Africa and to improve the integrity of corporate managements. As laudable as these goals were, there could be little doubt that the plans undertook the campaigns at least partially in response to public—that is, political—pressure.

As an economist with a quasi-libertarian pedigree, Alan

Greenspan plainly was uncomfortable with the government's investing in the public securities markets. The commission he chaired had explicitly endorsed continuing the restriction of the trust fund to Treasury securities, calling the rule "proper and appropriate." The commission certified the interest rates collected by the fund to be "equitable" and tried to dispel the allegation that the reserves had been "spent for other purposes outside of the Social Security program."

This latter charge derived from a 1970 change in federal budget procedure that merged the Social Security trust fund balance with the general federal budget, as though they were both part of a single bank account. The so-called unified budget confused the public (and politicians, for that matter) about how the trust fund money was being invested and spent. Rightly so.

Until the administration of Lyndon Johnson, Social Security's surpluses and deficits had been reported separately from the rest of the government. Therefore it always had been crystal clear when, say, the general fund was running a deficit and Social Security a surplus, or vice versa. When Social Security needed a fiscal shoring-up, as it often did between 1940 and 1970, the distinction between the budgets gave the necessary transfers a transparent, formal appearance.

LBJ ended such separate accounting for several reasons, including a desire to use the Social Security surplus to reduce the general government deficit. Starting in fiscal 1970, the government reported one combined budget balance, netting Social Security's surplus or deficit against all other government accounts. While this yielded what economists considered to be a more accurate picture of the government's overall fiscal condition, it also suggested that the funds were commingled in a way that could make it easy for the country to lose track of who owed what to whom.

Having grappled with the consequences, including allegations that prior trust fund surpluses had been squandered or "stolen" by politicians, the Greenspan commission recommended the trust fund's removal from the unified budget. But this was one recommendation that the politicians in Congress opted to ignore, possibly because the political expedience of a prospectively growing Social Security surplus wasn't lost on them. Presidents and lawmakers alike soon became hooked on the Social Security trust fund. The government sold T-bonds to the Social Security system, in effect borrowing the surplus, and once the borrowed money was in hand, they spent it. The question is, what did they spend it on?

This is more than an academic issue. Indeed, it's fundamental to the very question of whether the trust fund is "real" and whether its claims on the government must be honored. To see why, let's consider a typical attack on the "IOUs" in the fund, this one from Thomas Sowell, a prominent conservative economist. "Those bonds in the Social Security 'trust fund' represent no tangible assets," he wrote in 2001. "Not houses, not factories, not cars, not trains."

If he is correct, maybe the money really has been willfully squandered or even stolen. But is he correct?

This question is sometimes cast as a debate over whether the Social Security trust fund adds to "national savings," a technical term related to how much capital the country has for productive investment, especially investment that benefits future generations.

Unfortunately, one dollar being indistinguishable from another, it's impossible to nail down precisely how the government deployed the money it borrowed from the Social Security system. But we can draw some conclusions by looking at how the federal government spent its money generally during the 1980s and 1990s.

When the buildup of the Social Security trust fund began after 1983, the government—that is, the federal government outside of Social Security—was running enormous deficits. The Reagan administration had cut income taxes, but instead of reducing government expenditures to match the loss in revenue, it had *increased* spending, especially on defense. (As hard as it might be to remember, these were the waning days of the cold war.)

To avert major tax increases and to reduce the apparent size of the budget deficit, the administration simply spent the borrowed money on regular budget items. From one vantage point, this was wasteful. It was hard to argue that Social Security's resources were systematically invested on long-term development, say through new federal spending on roads, bridges, schoolbuildings, or other infrastructure, because that spending didn't expand. Instead, as Schieber and Shoven put it, "the savings of one branch of the government [that is, Social Security] (was) exactly canceled out by the dissaving of the rest."

Seen from another angle, however, the spending from the trust fund did contribute to national savings, and profoundly.

Here's how: Spending the trust fund assets on general federal programs relieved presidents from Reagan to George W. Bush of pressure to raise income taxes. Keeping marginal tax rates low left more money in the hands of the well-to-do investing class, who pay the bulk of income taxes and are presumed to have put the spare cash to work. After all, according to orthodox Reaganite "trickle-down" theory, reducing the tax burden on the investing class is what spurs business creation and job growth. Indeed, to this day Reagan apologists maintain that the historic economic expansion and stock market boom of the Clinton era in the 1990s was fueled by the Reagan tax cuts of the 1980s.

This suggests that the surplus money extracted from payroll taxpayers since 1983 has indeed contributed mightily to the nation's wealth. Wealthy investors subsidized by less-wealthy payroll taxpayers have spent it on the houses, factories, cars, and trains whose existence Mr. Sowell questioned.

Now that it has been spent, the time is approaching for it to be paid back.

And thus we return to the second motive for claiming that the trust fund is merely a pile of IOUs that might as well be ignored.

It's important to keep in mind how the trust fund assets are expected to be used a few decades from now. According to the Social Security system's official actuarial projection, the cost of benefits may start to exceed revenues from the payroll tax and interest at some point around 2021 or 2022. By then, the trust fund will own about $5.3 trillion in government securities. To raise cash to cover the shortfall, the program will start selling its bonds back to the government. (This is not a new option, remember; it was the whole point of parking billions of dollars a year in surplus funds with the U.S. Treasury.) Cashing in the whole reserve will take about 20 years.

Although this process may, on the surface, resemble transferring money from one pocket to another in the same pair of trousers, the reality is more complicated. That's because Social Security payroll taxes are fundamentally different from income taxes. Although most Americans pay both, the sets of income taxpayers and payroll taxpayers aren't identical.

For one thing, the distribution of the tax burden differs from one to the other: The payroll tax is regressive, meaning it costs lower-earning workers proportionately more than it costs the rich. The income tax is progressive, falling most heavily on higher-earning taxpayers. About three-quarters of all taxpayers, in fact, pay more Social Security tax than income tax. Since the payroll tax is only levied on the first $90,000 in earned income, taxpayers reap larger and larger payroll tax exemptions as their income rises above that amount—but they incur higher *income* tax rates as their income mounts.

The implications of this pattern may be clearer if, rather than view everyone as a contributor to both tax regimes, we view payroll taxpayers and income taxpayers seperately. Let's say Sam pays only Social Security tax, and Ingrid pays only income tax. (We'll ignore for now that most people are a mix of Sam and Ingrid.)

Since 1983, when Social Security taxes were increased and the buildup in the trust fund began, Sam has been paying more into the Social Security system than it has required to pay for current retirees' benefits. The excess has been funneled into the trust fund as a cushion against the baby-boom retirements. Until the money is needed to pay for those benefits, it is lent to the federal government, which has used it to cover general (that is, non–Social Security) expenses.

Considering that Ingrid's income taxes normally would be used to pay for those expenses, she has benefited from the transfer. Indeed, she and her fellow income tax filers have reaped a windfall of more than $1.5 trillion since 1983. Without the loans from Sam and his fellow Social Security taxpayers, her taxes would have been raised substantially. So she has been able to hold onto a larger proportion of her earnings since 1983 than she otherwise would have.

According to Social Security's official projections, the flow of money from the trust fund to the general budget will reverse course sometime around 2022. At that point, Ingrid will be obliged to repay the loans from Sam.

What will happen if she reneges on the loans? The options are not pleasant—but the unpleasantness is all visited on Sam. His Social Security benefits will have to be cut, or his payroll taxes will have to be raised. In either case, Ingrid will have enjoyed the fruits of Sam's tax payments for some 40 years. But he will have gained nothing—and he'll have to pay much more for his retirement, to boot.

It's true that repaying the loans without reducing the general federal budget may require an income tax increase—but that's a burden on Ingrid. In other words, the income tax may have to be raised to repay Ingrid's obligations to Sam. But isn't that the proper course?

The point made most commonly about the fiscal retrenchment the country might have to undergo to cover the trust fund redemptions is that it will, essentially, break the bank—that the necessary tax increases or budget cuts will be so large the economy will collapse. As Charles Krauthammer put it in the column quoted above, "The only relevant question . . . is whether, when the time comes to pay off, the federal government will be able to honor those IOUs."

Krauthammer should stop worrying.

The sums the government will have to transfer to Social Security, compared to the size of the economy at the time, should be manageable. Assuming that the gross domestic product grows at an average 4.5 percent a year in accordance with forecasts by the Congressional Budget Office, then the annual redemptions of trust fund assets will range from less than one-tenth of 1 percent of GDP in the 2020s (when the system will redeem the first set of bonds) up to a maximum of 2.65 percent of GDP by the 2040s. On average, the total of redemptions from 2025 through 2041 will come to less than one-half of one percent of GDP per year.

To look at this from another angle, the drawdown of the trust fund will peak between the years 2035 and 2040 according to the intermediate case projections of the Social Security actuaries. In that period, the difference between the cost of scheduled benefits and the revenues raised from the payroll tax will require redeeming about $700 billion a year of the trust fund's bonds.

By 2035, however, the entire federal budget will be nearly $9 trillion. It will expand to $11 trillion in 2040 (assuming the budget grows at the same projected rate as the U.S. economy). That suggests that the redemptions as a percentage of the federal budget will range from just over 7 percent to just over 6 percent. That's certainly not enough to justify wild claims by Social Security's critics that the redemptions would require tax increases of 50 percent.

It's hard to make the case that paying off the trust fund obligations would be a devastating blow to the economy. All we can say for sure is that if it's so, then President Bush's 2001–2003 tax cuts will be an even harsher blow. They're going to cost an average of 1.95 percent of GDP, or nearly four times the average cost of redeeming Social Security's assets.

In fact, the share of the tax cuts paid to the wealthiest 1 percent of Americans alone—those who, not so coincidentally, gained most from the government's borrowings from the Social Security trust fund in the first place—comes to about one-half of 1 percent of GDP. In other words, if their tax cuts were rolled back, the revenue gain to the government would cover the cost of redeeming the bonds, with a little bit left over. Maybe that's why, when you examine who is really behind the organizations lobbying for the privatization of Social Security, you find some of these same people.

Chapter Seven

Reform Comes Unstuck

THE 1983 REFORMS mapped out by the Greenspan commission seemed so successful at fixing Social Security's long-term problems that the commission's members spent several years basking in the glory. Among them was New York's learned and colorful Democratic senator, Daniel Patrick Moynihan. He could barely stop bragging about the commission's clever finesse of the baby-boom retirements—charging the maturing generation more in payroll tax than was needed to cover current retirees, and banking the excess. Thanks to an improving economy, the payroll tax was filling the program's reserve tanks even faster than anyone had forecast.

"Boy," Moynihan crowed, "we did better than we even realized."

"He was very enthusiastic about it," his co-commissioner Bob Ball recalled for an interviewer. "In fact, he wrote about it as if he had discovered it."

His glee soon faded. With the arrival of the first Bush administration, the mercurial Moynihan discovered the flaw buried deep in the commission's artful reform: the money accumulating in the trust fund created a mesmerizing temptation for politicians. As he watched George H. W. Bush siphon billions of dollars from the Social Security reserve into the federal rathole, just so he could mollify his conservative base by keeping his "read my lips" no-tax pledge, Moynihan's disillusionment ripened into outrage.

Over the previous few years, the income tax had been reduced for the richest Americans and Social Security taxes had gone up, mostly for middle- and lower-wage earners. But the goal of the Greenspan commission had been to strengthen Social Security, not enable presidents to claim budget-balancing victories.

Foreseeing the danger that the Social Security assets, once appropriated by the government, might never be recovered, Moynihan in 1990 sounded the alarm at what he called "outright thievery." Early that year, he introduced a bill to pare the payroll levy back to only what was needed to cover each year's benefits, thus placing temptation beyond the reach of the executive branch. This earned him a peevish rebuke from Bush. The President described Moynihan's measure, implausibly, as an attempt to cut benefits, and claimed that his own opposition to the bill proved his commitment to "protecting the sanctity" of the program. Congress, itself hooked on Social Security's revenues, refused to follow Moynihan's lead.

Notwithstanding the government's appetite for the Social Security reserve, the 1983 reforms turned out to have a different long-term problem. The new concern wasn't that they produced too much money, but not enough. By 1985, the Social Security actuaries had shifted their estimate of the trust fund's exhaustion date, which the Greenspan commission had pegged at 2063, sharply forward to 2049. Every year that passed brought the critical date two years closer; by 1995, the fund was expected to last only until 2029. This date was especially alarming, because it suggested that the reserves wouldn't even last long enough to cover the youngest baby boomers, who would be turning 65 that year.

The country had been promised that the tax increases and benefit adjustments of 1983 would bring Social Security into long-range fiscal equilibrium—that revenues and expenditures would balance over the customary 75-year projection period. The fix had been billed as permanent, or at least good enough to last three-quarters of a century. But by 1995, the projected long-range deficit had soared to 2.17 percent of taxable payroll, meaning that rebalancing the Social Security budget at that point would require a further increase in the payroll tax rate from 12.4 percent to nearly 14.6 percent. Not only had the fix failed, but the system was in much *worse* long-term condition than it had been in 1983.

The "popular explanation" for the deficit, as a 1996 Social Security advisory report observed, blamed it on the changing ratio of workers to beneficiaries. Whereas the ratio was 16:1 in 1950, by the mid-1980s there were only 3.3 workers paying into the system for every beneficiary; by 2040, when all the baby boomers had reached retirement age, there might be fewer than 2.0. Seen from that angle, it was easy to understand why Social Security seemed destined to become more expensive as time passed.

But the 1996 report debunked this explanation. The change in the ratio had "almost nothing to do with" the emerging deficit, it observed. In fact, the ratio hadn't budged at all between 1983 and 1994—it had stayed put at 3.3. Moreover, the projected decline to 2.0 or less had been taken fully into account in the 1983 reforms, which were designed to build a reserve fund precisely to protect the smaller population of workers from over-burdening when the boomers started retiring.

A closer look at the worker-beneficiary ratio is perhaps in order. The persistent misconceptions about the ratio's significance have proved harder to kill than Rasputin. Although it is largely irrelevant to the long-range deficit going forward, privatization advocates still trot it out as a scare tactic to rationalize radical changes to the system. A chart depicting the plummeting ratio in four-color graphics is part of the multimedia presentation that accompanies President Bush and other administration spokespersons at all their Social Security events.

But as an indicator of the system's overall health, this is a red herring. What the chart leaves out is that the most dramatic decline in the ratio took place in the first few decades of Social Security's existence, when millions of workers were paying payroll taxes but only a small number had begun to collect retirement benefits. Between 1940 and 1965, the ratio plummeted from 16 to 1 to about 4 to 1, the fastest decline in the program's history, but one that did not place any great strain on the program's financial condition. By 1984 the ratio was down to about 3.3 to 1, where it remained for more than 10 years. Since then it has declined modestly, and will continue to do so as the large baby-boom generation enters retirement and the so-called baby-bust generation remains in the workforce.

But there are some indications that the worker-beneficiary ratio may plateau or even improve after the boomer retirements run their course. One scenario mapped out by the Social Security actuaries shows the ratio never dipping below 2.3 to 1, and rising to 2.4 to 1 after 2045. Among the factors that could affect the ratio are an increase in immigration (including illegal immigration), a rise in the fertility rate of American women (one possible result of higher immigration), or a slowing of increases in life expectancy (conceivable if medical advances begin to yield diminishing benefits).

The long-term deficit that appeared in the 1990s arose from several other factors. Changes in economic assumptions, including the actuaries' newly pessimistic view of the rate of future wage growth, accounted for half of the shortfall. A faulty projection of disability expenses, which were coming in much higher than expected, accounted for another third. The incorporation of new demographic statistics, especially a set concerning immigrants' working patterns, accounted for most of the rest.

That such incremental adjustments could result in a major miscalculation attested to the folly of placing too much faith in the accuracy of the 75-year projection. Ball, among others, had been pressing that point for years. But the miscalculation nevertheless caused great dismay. For the third time in less than 25 years, a major fiscal repair had come unstuck. The 1972 amendments, which included the exuberant 20 percent benefit increase, had been knocked off kilter by the first Arab oil embargo and the inflation double-indexing fiasco. The damage supposedly had been mended by Jimmy Carter's straitened reforms in 1977. Those hadn't done the job, so the task of reestablishing the system's stability for the future had been dumped on the Greenspan commission. And now, the program was back at square one yet again.

Economists and lawmakers started to wonder whether some fundamental structural weakness in Social Security might require tax hikes and benefit cuts stretching endlessly into the future, turning the program into a voracious consumer of the national wealth. The decade from the mid-1980s to the mid-1990s was the period in which doubts about Social Security's survival really took hold. The cry, "Will it be there for me?" symbolized what appeared to be a profound inequity dividing the older generations of recipients from their children and grandchildren. The first beneficiaries collected generous stipends despite their meager contributions; their offspring were saddled with higher payroll taxes and a dubious return. The doubts were stoked by the increasingly well-organized privatization lobby, led by the Cato Institute and the Heritage Foundation, which in 1983 had conceived the strategy of chipping away at the system's public support by sowing distrust among younger workers. By 1995, their plan looked remarkably prescient.

There was no question that Social Security needed more patching. As the first baby-boomer president, Bill Clinton belonged to the generation that first came to doubt whether Social Security would play the role in their lives that it had for their forebears. As an heir to the Democratic legacy of FDR, he might have taken the issue personally in hand, rebuilding its defenses against the ideologues who were determined to raze the last remaining edifice of the New Deal. Instead, his administration would oversee the most inept attempt to fix the system in 25 years—one that left it more vulnerable to enemy assault than it had ever been before.

Until the late 1990s, the executive branch was required to appoint a Social Security advisory council every four years to consider, rather like a county grand jury, whatever issues happened to arise during its tenure. Midway through Clinton's first term, the clock ticked over.

For all the concern in the air about the system's fiscal condition, the 13 members of the 1994 advisory council took office without receiving a specific brief for reform. The problems were all on the long-term side, and if there's any hard-and-fast rule governing agendas in Washington, it's that long-term problems end up on the back burner.

The Clinton White House seemed to have selected the council members through some absentminded lottery. Ball complained later that in making the appointments the administration seemed more intent on achieving a fashionable ideal of "diversity" than on assembling a group of committed, knowledgeable, and politically astute experts. The council included one Hispanic, an African American, five women, three labor representatives, and two corporate executives—on paper, indeed, it looked perfectly balanced. But it lacked focus and urgency. Ball, who had come to believe that his stature as a former Social Security chief and a key figure on the Greenspan commission warranted virtually an automatic appointment, had to lobby hard to secure his own nomination. ("They really didn't know how to turn me down when I made clear that I would like to be on it," he recalled.)

Ball didn't think highly of the appointed chairman, Edward Gramlich, a liberal economist and dean of the School of Public Policy at the University of Michigan. (Clinton later named him a governor of the Federal Reserve Board, where at this writing he is still serving under Alan Greenspan.) "Gramlich was a quite typical academician," Ball recalled sourly. In Ball's long experience, advisory commissions always saw their mission as producing a blueprint for congressional action, but Gramlich "ran this thing like an advanced seminar in graduate school. He wanted to be sure he examined all the possibilities, and he thought that everyone had an equal claim on the truth." To Ball, a Social Security lifer who had been fending off the program's enemies for nearly a half-century, this was a perverse, even dangerous notion. If Gramlich really intended to reexamine first principles in a kind of academic exercise, he thought, no good could come of it.

The setup didn't necessarily please those who supported such a reexamination, either. Sylvester Schieber, an executive at the corporate consulting firm Watson Wyatt, later groused that the council ended up so "hopelessly divided in its recommendations" that his own innovative proposal for privatizing the program never received the consideration it deserved.

Under Gramlich's languid hand, the council fragmented into three antagonistic camps. Ball's camp, which would stand against any proposal to curb benefits, was composed of Edith Fierst, a pension lawyer; Thomas W. Jones, president of TIAA-CREF, the big pension plan for college and school faculty members; and the three union representatives. Schieber and Carolyn Weaver, a conservative former member of Bob Dole's Senate staff, recruited three other members, including Fidel Vargas, the ambitious mayor of a small southern California city and, at 25, the youngest member of the council, to join their campaign to place private accounts on the council agenda. Gramlich ended up in the middle, and from here he tried to pursue a doomed strategy of placating the factions on both his flanks.

Ball gave up early on reaching an accord with Schieber or Weaver, whom he had pegged as "an ideologue and an unrelenting critic of Social Security." Instead, he concentrated on holding at bay any endorsement of privatization by a majority of the council—indeed, on quashing any suggestion that the fundamental social-insurance role of the program was subject to debate.

Without any clear direction from the White House, it was probably inevitable that the council would break apart over the basic issue of whether Social Security should continue to perform a social insurance function. This was a profound question that required thorough and transparent public debate and by the careful scrutiny of a blue-ribbon panel. A group with the stature of the Greenspan commission, composed of senators, congresspersons, corporate presidents, and union leaders, might have been able to handle it, but not this largely anonymous group. After nearly two years of work wracked by unbridgeable ideological disagreement, the council produced three incompatible reform proposals, practically guaranteeing that nothing would come of its labors in politically fractious Washington.

Ball's clique produced an eight-point package they labeled the "maintain benefits" plan and that Schieber derided as the usual "Chinese menu" of marginal tweaks. Among the familiar old ideas in the package were extending mandatory Social Security coverage to all new state and local government employees; increasing the taxation of benefits; raising the payroll tax rate for employers and employees by 0.8 percent each, starting in the comfortably remote year 2045; and increasing the number of years of work used to calculate average lifetime wages to 38 from 35, a change that would generally reduce initial benefits because the additional years would be clustered in the early, low-paid end of a worker's career. Ball added one new idea: Allowing the trust fund to invest in common stocks, with a goal of shifting 40 percent of the reserve into equities by 2015. With the possible exception of the provision to change the lifetime wage formula, Ball could safely argue that he had held the line against a benefit cut.

At the opposite end of the spectrum was Schieber's "personal security account" scheme. By any measure, this would place Social Security on an entirely new course. Its centerpiece was the transformation of the program's basic benefit into a flat payment of $410 a month for everybody, regardless of wage history or economic class. This sum would mean a roughly 30 percent cut from the average monthly stipend at the time and would amount to less than two-thirds of the federal poverty level for an individual.

To make up for such a draconian cut in guaranteed benefits, 5 percentage points of every worker's payroll tax, or almost the entire employee contribution of 6.2 percent, would be diverted into tax-exempt private accounts. Schieber later calculated the cost of transforming Social Security from a pay-as-you-go system into his program at about $2 trillion, which he proposed to borrow from the U.S. government and repay once the system reached fiscal stability sometime after 2034.

To a staunch defender of traditional Social Security like Ball, the sole virtue in Schieber's plan was that its radical novelty reduced its chances of public acceptance almost to zero. Although it had attracted almost as many supporters on the council as his own, five members to six, Ball viewed it more as a "stalking horse" for the generic idea of private accounts than a credible proposal.

He was much more uneasy about Gramlich's plan, a pared-down privatization scheme that appeared on the surface to require merely a judicious tinkering with Social Security's funding. Like Schieber's proposal, Gramlich's "individual accounts" scheme, or IA in council shorthand, achieved about half of its projected savings by cutting benefits sharply. But the cuts were progressive, ranging from zero for the poorest workers to an initial 30 percent for the wealthiest. On the private account side, Gramlich proposed to require that all workers contribute an additional 1.6 percent of wages, over and above the 6.2 percent payroll tax, into tax-exempt retirement accounts.

Gramlich thought that with a modicum of political finesse the additional 1.6 percent levy might be sold to the public as an investment in personal nest eggs rather than a "tax," but he was philosophical about its chances. "Frankly, I knew this measure would not be popular," he acknowledged after the advisory council ended its deliberations. But he had long been concerned about workers' tendency to undersave for retirement, and thought the IA plan was a promising way to coerce people, especially lower-earning workers, to start building a postcareer cushion.

Because the Schieber and Gramlich proposals both reduced the proportion of retirement income that would come from a guaranteed monthly stipend, they undermined Social Security's goal of shielding the working class from the vicissitudes and risks of life. Instead of insulating workers from the ebb and flow of the economic cycle, private accounts loaded them with risk. Those fortunate enough to build their accounts during flush times in the stock market might have comfortable retirements, but those whom the market gods didn't favor would be condemned to greater reliance on the meager basic benefit.

The council ended its work in 1996, deeply split. Some members regretted for years that they had failed to produce a blueprint for Social Security's future. Schieber, judging from the tone of the book he coauthored about Social Security reform, resented Ball's tireless efforts to frustrate any consideration of private accounts. Ball, for his part, understood that at some level he had been outmaneuvered: the Schieber and Gramlich proposals had placed the privatization of Social Security, if abstractly, on the domestic policy table.

At the White House, however, Ball did manage to have the last word. At his urging, Clinton endorsed a plan to allow Social Security to invest in corporate equities. He also proposed transferring money directly from the healthy federal surplus that had accumulated during his administration to the program to shore up its finances. In a nod to the concept of private accounts, Clinton also proposed a new program of tax-subsidized and government-matched retirement accounts, for which only lower-income workers would be eligible. These accounts, significantly, were to be funded by additional contributions from the workers and the government, not by money diverted from Social Security.

Gramlich, for his part, later acknowledged that Clinton's proposal "might be more palatable politically" than his own. But he observed that existing voluntary plans, such as individual retirement accounts and 401(k) accounts, never managed to achieve more than 40 percent participation among lower-income workers. "Voluntary is voluntary," he said, regretfully.

In any event, nothing ever came of the Clinton package. Clinton was a lame duck, his presidency marked more than anything else by its unfulfilled potential. It would be up to a President Gore to follow through. Indeed, Gore made the safeguarding of Social Security (expressed via his oft-ridiculed "lockbox" analogy) a key plank of his presidential campaign against Texas governor George W. Bush.

But there would be no President Gore taking office in 2001. Instead, there was a Republican president. By 2002, George W. Bush would turn the record $230-billion surplus recorded in the last year of the Clinton administration into a $158-billion deficit, largely through the mechanism of a spendthrift tax cut. Rather than safeguard Social Security, he set out to destroy it. As one of his first acts upon taking office, he appointed his own Social Security commission and instructed it to come up with whatever plan it could to mend the program's finances—any plan, that is, as long as it required no payroll tax increase whatsoever and endorsed the creation of private retirement accounts. The commission members had been carefully screened to make sure they came to the table predisposed to follow the president's vision. The privatization lobby, at last, was inside the gates.

Chapter Eight

The Privateers

T HEY BEAR unexceptionable, reassuring, even uplifting names, like the National Taxpayers Union, the Center for Freedom and Prosperity, FreedomWorks, and the Alliance for Worker Retirement Security—who could be opposed to that? They sponsor websites whose warm comfort-food titles, such as retiresafe.org and retiresecure.org, are belied by the alarmed tone within, sounding the warning that the collapse of Social Security is inevitable and offering the one true path to its salvation: diverting workers' contributions into private investment accounts.

And they parrot the promise emanating from the Bush White House—that private accounts will do more than protect retirees' lifestyles; they'll make them and their families wealthy beyond their wildest dreams.

As retiresafe.org, the website of the Council for Government Reform (and who doesn't favor government reform?) puts it:

"How would you like to retire a millionaire? Leave your children a nest egg? Become a stakeholder in the American economy?

"Personal retirement accounts are the answer."

Dozens of such organizations have collected beneath one big tent in the name of privatizing Social Security. As the plot against Social Security unfolds, they are spending lavishly on issue advertising, drawing from a slush fund of as much as $200 million raised with the help of White House operatives. Like a fleet of Revolutionary-era privateers, sailing under private flags but doing the work of the powers in government, they operate through deception, distraction, and disguise.

They profess to speak directly for the millions of enrollees with a stake in the program's survival, whether as contributors, beneficiaries, or the parents and grandparents of future beneficiaries. USA Next (formerly the United Seniors Association), whose "national chairman" is the venerable and folksy Art Linkletter, identifies itself as a "a nationwide 1.5 million-plus citizens activist network." The National Taxpayers Union stands up "first, last and always for the rights of people who pay for our government." FreedomWorks congratulates itself for deploying "a growing and permanent volunteer grassroots army."

But these organizations aren't grassroots so much as astroturf—artificial versions of the real thing. While they claim to be protecting the interests of the disenfranchised, they're really fronts for the wealthy and powerful. The same well-heeled and well-connected contributors appear over and over again on their donor lists—major corporations, banks, insurance companies, and Wall Street securities firms; right-wing foundations and think tanks; conservative religious leaders; and political operatives (usually Republican).

Staff and board members float from one to another as easily

as retired politicians move from Congress to Washington trade organizations and lobbying firms. Their more talented and articulate staffers are just as skilled at slipping through the capital's revolving door, bouncing from stints on congressional subcommittee staffs and White House task groups to the astroturf lobby and back again, like a roving Delta Force of youthful ideologues.

Consider Andrew Biggs, a young economist educated at Cambridge University and the London School of Economics. A sandy-haired, self-confident 37, Biggs began his Washington career on the staff of the House Banking and Financial Services Subcommittee, then moved to the libertarian Cato Institute (perhaps the most prominent promoter of privatization in the country), where he served as a Social Security analyst. His next stop was the staff of President Bush's 2001 Commission to Strengthen Social Security, which placed three schemes to privatize Social Security on the legislative drawing board. Biggs's supervisor there was Charles Blahous, the commission's executive director. Blahous, who had previously been executive director of the Alliance for Worker Retirement Security, a front for the National Association of Manufacturers devoted to privatizing Social Security, would parlay his commission post into a job at the White House, where he is currently President Bush's point man on the reform campaign.

Let's not lose track of Biggs. After working for the commission, he briefly returned to Cato before landing at the Social Security Administration itself, where he has been serving as associate commissioner for retirement policy since 2003. In that capacity, he shared the stage with President Bush at the January 11 "real people" panel discussion on Social Security's future. President Bush identified Biggs that morning as an "expert," as well he might.

Washington brims with so many such nimble young "experts" that the press sometimes loses track of them. In December 2004, the *CBS Evening News* covered the developing battle over Social Security through an interview with one Tad De-Haven, 28, whom it labeled "the poster child for Social Security reform."

"I don't expect to get anything from Social Security," De-Haven obligingly informed the camera. "It's not going to be there." He did express some interest in owning a private account, however.

What the segment failed to mention was that DeHaven had been a staff member at both the Cato Institute and the Heritage Foundation, another right-wing think tank, before joining the National Taxpayers Union as an economic policy analyst. All three organizations are sworn devotees of private accounts, a fact that evidently escaped the reporters and editors at CBS News.

The astroturf organizations that employ people like Biggs, Blahous, and DeHaven share a libertarian agenda that encompasses reducing taxation, constraining government regulations, and promoting what they choose to call family values. Since the 1980s, the cause that unites them more than any other is the reform of Social Security.

How the nation's social insurance system became a glue holding together elements of the New Right, the Republican right, business and industry, and the evangelical Christian movement is not hard to understand, considering how neatly their agendas overlap.

The insurance and investment industries see Social Security reform as a source of profit, on the expectation that billions of dollars in management fees will flow their way if private retirement accounts become a reality. Reform also fits the agendas of groups that believe there's nothing the government does that private enterprise can't do better, as well as libertarian organizations that believe there's very little government should do, period.

Anti-government ideologues, meanwhile, view the dismantling of Social Security, the biggest government program of all, as a symbolic blow against an inflated public sector. This suits industrialists who chafe under the thumb of government regulators; it's no accident that oilmen subject to costly environmental oversight and ranchers subject to irksome restrictions on access to government land are among the most generous contributors to libertarian think tanks and pressure groups. It also suits religious moralists, who believe that government programs spread a secular morality.

Tax "reformers," who see all government levies as dead weights on the free market (the National Taxpayers Union says its goals are to "scrap the current tax code" and "shut down the IRS") are naturally unhappy with the Social Security payroll tax and the program's aim to redistribute wealth; a system of private accounts, by definition, would be incompatible with income redistribution. Free-market advocates see great virtue in allowing—even requiring—workers to take responsibility for their own retirements instead of relying on the government to assure their old-age security. Big employers fear that the retention of the existing Social Security system will mean an increase in the payroll tax, which would cost business an extra $50 million for every percentage point increase.

Just as an opera diva hires a claque of fawning admirers to jump-start the applause after her aria, the Bush administration has relied on these groups for assistance with its Social Security privatization campaign. The astroturf lobbies provide the administration with legal cover, enabling White House aides to raise a war chest from corporate and individual donors without naming the sources—money to spread the gospel of privatization and the ownership society, produce and distribute issue ads to television networks, and deploy platoons of ostensibly nonpartisan analysts to news media.

The most important lobbying groups fall into three main categories.

First is the ideological vanguard, represented by the Heritage Foundation, founded in 1973, and the Cato Institute, founded in 1977. Sometimes it is hard to determine where one ends and the other begins; the seminal strategic manifesto of the privatization movement written by two Heritage analysts in 1983 was published in the *Cato Journal*.

Heritage and Cato have provided a sort of intellectual foundation for the privatization movement. Their staff members publish widely, sponsor Washington conferences that bring together leading economists and policy makers, and work effectively with Congress and the White House. Most of the more carefully argued tracts that appear on the websites of astroturf groups are likely to carry a Heritage or Cato pedigree.

They share more than a free-market libertarian agenda. Their sources of financial backing closely overlap, too. Heritage was established with money from Joseph Coors, a conservative Colorado beer magnate, and Richard Mellon Scaife, an heir to the Mellon industrial fortune who took his family's philanthropic foundations on a distinctly rightward veer in the 1970s. Much of Cato's initial funding came from the Koch family, a passel of conservative Kansas oilmen. The Koch patriarch, Fred Koch, was a cofounder of the John Birch Society.

In later years, both organizations received generous funding from the Koch family, Coors, Scaife, and the John M. Olin Foundation, a conservative foundation based on a chemical manufacturing fortune. In recent years, Cato has also begun to tap into a pool of corporate donors, including the financial powerhouses American Express and Citicorp, pharmaceutical giants such as Merck and Pfizer, and the oil conglomerates ExxonMobil and ChevronTexaco.

The next circle of proselytizers is composed of industry front groups. Among the most senior of these is the Alliance for Worker Retirement Security, sponsor of the website retiresecure.org. The Alliance was founded in the 1990s by Cato alumna Leanne Abdnor as an arm of the National Association of Manufacturers, whose Washington quarters it shares to this day. Its executive director, the prolific editorialist Derrick A. Max, is another alumnus of Cato, where he helped lead the institute's campaign for Social Security privatization.

The Alliance currently boasts a membership of more than 40 corporations and business lobbying groups, including the American Bankers Association, the Business Roundtable, the U.S. Chamber of Commerce, Hewlett-Packard, the pharmaceutical company Pfizer, and the securities firm PaineWebber.

Although these supporters were once proud to have their names listed on retiresecure.org, they have recently suffered an attack of mass modesty. In February 2005, the brokerage firm Edward D. Jones & Co. withdrew from the alliance, of which it had been a founding member. The move followed picketing by the AFL-CIO at several Jones offices. A few days later, Pfizer announced it was taking a neutral stance on privatization—possibly because AARP, the huge advocacy group for seniors, pointed out that its membership accounted for a significant share of the customer base for prescription pharmaceuticals. Soon after that, the roster listing the corporate and trade members of the Alliance vanished from retiresecure.org, leaving no trace.

Another group, Citizens for a Sound Economy, was founded in 1984 by the Koch family. Over the following decade, CSE rose to political prominence under the leadership of C. Boyden Gray, a former White House counsel to President George H. W. Bush. CSE perfected a strategy of accepting corporate donations to campaign for the donors' pet political issues. As the *Washington Post* reported in 2000, the group accepted more than $1 million from Philip Morris "at a time when CSE was opposing cigarette taxes," large contributions from Exxon while denigrating the concept of global warming as "junk science," and donations from Microsoft, which was facing a worrisome federal antitrust lawsuit, to lobby for cuts in the Department of Justice's antitrust budget.

In 2004, CSE merged with Empower America, a conservative political action group cofounded by former representative Jack F. Kemp and former U.S. Education secretary William J. Bennett, forming FreedomWorks to lobby for the "Freedom Agenda"— for private retirement accounts, a flat tax, and school vouchers.

Empower America exemplifies another category of astroturf lobbies: front groups for the White House and political partisans. The epitome of these is Progress for America. Although it identifies itself as a "national grassroots organization," the group is inextricably associated with Bush political guru Karl Rove and heavily funded by such financial services corporations as Ameriquest Capital ($5 million in contributions during the 2004 election cycle), the insurance conglomerate American Financial Group ($1.5 million), and Charles Schwab. In 2002, as Bush started to plan his reelection campaign, the *Washington Post* quoted Tony Feather, a Bush-Cheney campaign official who was one of the group's officers, as describing the organization as "simply a vehicle for building grassroots support for Bush's policies."

Finally, there are organizations that cross multiple lines. Perhaps one of the most peculiar is USA Next, formerly known as the United Seniors Association. USA Next has tried to establish itself as an alternative to AARP by staking out diametrically opposite positions on Social Security and Medicaid. Although the avuncular Art Linkletter is the organization's figurehead, its real chief is Charles W. Jarvis, a walking illustration of how the multiple threads of astroturf lobbying are braided together.

The pugnacious Jarvis is a former Reagan administration official, former executive of a waste management company, and former aide-de-camp to Dr. James Dobson, the family-values evangelizer who made headlines in 2005 by accusing the cartoon character SpongeBob SquarePants of secretly proselytizing for a gay lifestyle. Jarvis also served in the abortive 2000 presidential campaign of the right-wing Christian activist Gary L. Bauer.

His organization has an even more distinguished right-wing pedigree. United Seniors Association was founded in 1991 by Richard A. Viguerie, the pioneer of New Right direct-mail campaigns. When Jarvis took over as chairman and CEO in 2001, he aligned the group with a first-class sugar daddy—the pharmaceutical industry. Using multimillion-dollar "educational" grants from Pharmaceutical Research and Manufacturers of America, the huge lobbying group known as PhRMA, and other industry fronts, USA spent nearly $10 million on an ad campaign in favor of a Medicare prescription drug plan designed around private-account principles.

The work gave USA valuable experience in how to provide a "veneer of 'seniors' legitimacy" to a political and corporate agenda. Throughout the Medicare prescription campaign, Jarvis gave numerous interviews, insisting that his ad project was a "grassroots" campaign serving the best interests of its constituency. He claimed that USA had a membership roll of more than a million senior citizens, although the organization's federal income tax returns generally reported no income whatsoever from membership dues and fees.

As USA morphed into USA Next, it promoted a curiously diverse platform. The two top items in the "Action Center" section of its website exhorted members to urge the Academy of Motion Picture Arts and Sciences not to deny an Oscar to Mel Gibson's movie *The Passion of the Christ* and to write their congressmen protesting the "government funding of AARP." (The misleading reference to "government funding" is to a Department of Labor work-training program for poverty-stricken workers over 55, which is administered by AARP and 12 other national organizations.)

Meanwhile, the group ran afoul of the Social Security Administration, which fined USA more than $554,000 in 2003 for a junk-mail campaign using envelopes designed to gull their elderly recipients into believing they were official communications from Social Security headquarters. The ruling by an administrative law judge stated that USA "knew that it might be crossing a line" in sending out envelopes marked "Social Security Information Enclosed," because the Social Security Administration agency had vehemently objected to the mailing's design in advance.

Social Security officials, concerned that recipients fooled into opening USA's phony alerts would subsequently toss genuine agency communications into the trash, "struggled vainly to convince [USA] to curb its practice of sending potentially deceptive mailings to senior citizens," the judge observed. "It chose to ignore these warnings."

So much for USA Next's sanctimonious concern for the welfare of its "members."

As the president's privatization campaign gathered momentum in early 2005, USA Next positioned itself even more prominnently as the anti-AARP, as though it had been assigned the task of running interference for the White House against the most powerful anti-privatization organization in Washington. Jarvis told reporters that his group would spend $10 million on a campaign against AARP, which he labeled "the boulder in the middle of the highway to personal savings accounts."

As professional advisers he hired several managers of the infamous Swift Boat Vets campaign that had smeared Democratic presidential candidate John Kerry. Their first effort, an online ad placed on a conservative website and headlined "The Real AARP Agenda," accused AARP of failing to support American troops overseas and favoring gay marriage—a charge so extreme and repellent that even a key USA Next ally in the battle, the Cato Institute, attacked it as "bigoted." Facing a storm of outrage, USA withdrew the ad after a few days. But an acrid pall remained. The tone was set for the coming campaign.

One remarkable aspect of this extremely efficient network of lobbyists and ideologues is how far it has evolved from its 40-year-old roots.

The landslide defeat of Barry Goldwater in the 1964 presidential election is generally regarded as the nadir of the conservative movement. But the rout, followed as it was by Lyndon Johnson's aggressive promotion of his Great Society program, awakened a sleeping giant. Over the next two decades, the most important conservative and libertarian think tanks—the Catos and Heritages—appeared. They were sustained by money from wealthy entrepreneurs and industrial heirs who were determined to create counterparts to liberal philanthropies such as the Ford and Rockefeller foundations (which themselves had become rather more liberal than their own founders had ever been).

One of the wealthiest institutions among the new breed was the Pittsburgh-based Sarah Mellon Scaife Foundation. The Scaife customarily spent the income from its hundreds of millions of dollars in assets on "traditional community causes such as the opera and the United Negro College Fund," the *Washington Post* reported. Derived from the fortune of a family whose most prominent member had been Andrew Mellon, a Pittsburgh banker, philanthropist, and Treasury secretary under three Republican presidents (and the namesake of the auditorium where President Bush launched his campaign against Social Security in January), the foundation came under the leadership of Mrs. Scaife's reactionary son, Richard Mellon Scaife in the 1970s.

Richard Scaife soon focused the foundation and several other family trusts on furthering conservative ideology. He contributed so heavily to the Cato Institute, Heritage Foundation, and other like-minded institutions that the *Washington Post* called him, in a two-part 1999 profile, the "funding father of the Right." (By then he had achieved a form of infamy as the figure behind the more scurrilous attacks on the Clintons during the impeachment controversy, spearheading vicious probes into the Clintons' Arkansas business dealings, the death of White House aide Vincent Foster, and other issues.)

As the rightist think tanks became part of the Washington woodwork, they began to attract donations from corporations hoping to parlay their political influence into favorable action at the Capitol and the White House. What is now ExxonMobil, for example, generously supported Cato, Heritage, and the American Enterprise Institute. (To be sure, the company hedged its bets with donations to recipients on the opposite side of the political spectrum.) Prominent financial services firms joined them in cosponsoring conferences and symposiums devoted to restructuring the tax code and breaking down the edifice of financial market regulation that, like Social Security, had been a hallmark of the New Deal.

Given that the 1960s and 1970s marked the beginning of the U. S. religious and ideological culture wars—among other developments, the Supreme Court's 1973 opinion upholding abortion rights in *Roe v. Wade* placed a divisive religious and moral issue at the fulcrum of American politics—it is hardly surprising that the conservative network treated economic and social issues as different sides of the same coin. The Heritage Foundation's founding president, Paul Weyrich, could write equally impassioned screeds on behalf of free-market economics and against "incessant western rock music," "political correctness," and other supposed harbingers of American cultural decline. The other conservative organizations cast equally wide nets.

Meanwhile, a new brand of laissez-faire economics was emerging, with Milton Friedman as its prophet. In his books *Capitalism and Freedom* (1962) and *Free to Choose* (written with his wife, Rose, in 1980), Friedman lionized individual choice as the highest goal of the capitalist system. He maintained that government intervention in the free market, no matter how well intentioned, suppressed individual economic freedom. Taxation, public schooling, and government regulation all came in for their lumps in Friedman's work. But he harbored singular scorn for Social Security, which he argued should be entirely private and entirely voluntary. "I find it hard to justify requiring 100 percent of the people to adopt a government-prescribed straitjacket," he wrote in 1999, adding that when Barry Gold-water had advocated the conversion of Social Security to a voluntary system during the 1964 campaign, he had wholeheartedly agreed.

Friedman's economics became one of the guiding philosophies of the Reagan administration, even though the Reagan White House, which increased the federal government to unprecedented size, honored his precepts mostly in the breach. The chairman of Reagan's Council of Economic Advisers, Martin Feldstein, was another proponent of the free-market school. White House corridors teemed with libertarian tax cutters and enthusiastic program slashers. The creed of Social Security privatization, promoted until then by a tiny and unheeded but single-minded group of ideologues, began to spread.

The stock market boom that coincided with the arrival of the Clinton administration added fuel to the fire. What became the longest bull market in history seemed to justify in retrospect the Darwinian economic rhetoric of the Reagan years. The newsletters of conservative think tanks began to offer not only paeans to the free market, but proclamations of the riches to be gained from investing in stocks.

The boom years would give the privatization of Social Security an ineluctable allure. It was hard to take issue with the opportunities offered by a bull market that was producing average annual gains of 26 percent from 1995 through 1999. If the free-market ideologues and the financial industry had been better organized to exploit the public's investment mania before the boom came to its abrupt end in 2000, and if a determined enemy of Social Security had already been seated in the White House, the plot against the program might well have succeeded then and there.

But Social Security still retained its reputation as the third rail of domestic politics, and Bill Clinton was hardly the man to dismantle a treasured Democratic program. The privateers have lately been spreading a story that Clinton would have instituted private retirement accounts toward the end of his administration if he had not been foiled by the impeachment scandal. In fact, Clinton was indeed toying with the idea of expanding the opportunities for private retirement accounts, but his version would have offered them as an addition to Social Security benefits, not as a substitute.

The 2000 market bust ended the public's enchantment with stocks, if only temporarily. The blush came off the privatization idea. One obstacle to its popularization had always been the reluctance of Wall Street firms to put their brawny shoulders behind the concept. As tempting as the prospect of moving hundreds of millions of dollars of tax-generated capital out of Treasury securities and into corporate stocks and bonds might have been, the financial services industry was extremely wary of aligning itself against what was still the nation's most popular federal program. The new Bush administration was committed to privatizing Social Security, but as late as mid-2001, Wall Street was still on the sidelines.

Into the void stepped a small if not entirely obscure firm, the Frank Russell Company. Known chiefly as the creator of the Russell 5000 index, a barometer of small-capitalization stocks that had enjoyed a high profile during the boom, the company had established a global consulting business advising foreign governments on social insurance privatization schemes.

Russell assigned one of its globe-trotting executives, D. Don Ezra, to establish a business lobby to push the idea on these shores. Ezra promptly made contact with Social Security reformers in the White House. According to a report at the time, he began meeting in early 2001 with Larry Lindsey, the president's chief economic adviser, and Chuck Blahous, who was then serving his stint as executive director of Bush's hand-picked Social Security reform commission. Ezra later claimed to have been part of White House discussions on a timetable for privatization and even to have consulted on the formation of the commission itself.

In June 2001, Ezra's fledgling lobbying group, the Coalition for American Financial Security, scored a publicity coup at its own coming-out party. Invited as a keynote speaker to its first luncheon, held in Windows on the World, the top-floor restaurant of New York's World Trade Center, Treasury secretary Paul O'Neill obliged the organizers with an extemporaneous 30-minute attack on the system's finances. He displayed particular contempt for what he characterized as the fictional trust fund assets.

If corporate pension managers ran their funds like Social Security, he said, "we'd all be in jail" for having "obligations without assets behind them.

"Today we have no assets in the trust fund. We have promises of the good faith and credit of the United States government that benefits will flow." One reporter in the room noted that O'Neill's view, while "widely shared among Republicans," was remarkable, considering that as the chief trustee of the Social Security system, he had signed his name to the latest trustees report, which attested to its holdings of $900 billion in Treasury securities.

If no one else noticed that the highest-ranking fiscal officer of the United States government had just casually raised the prospect of a default on nearly $1 trillion in bonds backed by its full faith and credit, it was just as well. With another $3.6 trillion in such bonds then outstanding around the world, the consequences might have included global financial turmoil.

It's not clear whether O'Neill's speech was specifically sanctioned by the White House or merely reflected his blunt-spoken personality. One way or another, his remarks boosted both the cause of privatization and the stature of the newly formed coalition.

Within a few months, however, events beyond the group's control placed Social Security reform on the back burner. In the aftermath of the 9/11 attacks, the White House became preoccupied with domestic security and war to the exclusion of almost everything else.

But the work of Ezra's organization and the presidential commission built a strong foundation for what would become the top priority of George Bush's second term. Even before Inauguration Day 2005, the White House front group Progress for America had started preparations for an all-out fundraising effort on behalf of privatization by calling quietly for multimillion-dollar contributions from corporate backers.

Its first public effort, a television ad on CNN and the Fox News Channel comparing Bush's plans for Social Security favorably to the system's founding by Franklin D. Roosevelt, didn't go well. The ad paired a film clip of FDR at the 1935 signing ceremony for the Social Security Act with a clip featuring President Bush. ("It took courage to create Social Security," the voiceover intoned. "It will take courage and leadership to protect it.") The ad enraged FDR's grandson, James Roosevelt Jr., himself a former Social Security executive, who proclaimed that his grandfather would "surely oppose" the Bush proposals. Roosevelt demanded that the group "cease using my grandfather's image." Rather than apologize and withdraw the commercial, Progress for America unabashedly left it on the air.

As the privatization drive took off in earnest, the astroturf lobbies coalesced into a formidable strike force. The Alliance for Worker Retirement Security's Derrick Max took on the important new assignment of coordinating a new umbrella group to succeed Ezra's short-lived coalition. Max's group was dubbed the Coalition for the Modernization and Protection of America's Social Security, or CoMPASS, and it set a high bar for itself—raising more than $20 million from corporate sponsors to promote privatization.

CoMPASS and Progress for America provided valuable shelter for financial services companies that were still wary of becoming identified directly with a historic reform, but thirsted for the gold. ("Most people in the business are keeping a very low profile . . . because of the potential backlash," one industry executive told the *Los Angeles Times*.) All the companies had to do was put up the cash, and the political operators would take it from there.

Chapter Nine

The Ownership Scam I: Risk or Reward?

O NE MIGHT SAY that the mark of a truly terrible idea is that it outlasts the delusions that first gave it life.

The notion that Social Security will be saved from financial ruin by converting it wholly or partially into a system of private investment accounts goes back at least a quarter-century. This was the era that gave us supply-side economics, the "trickle-down" justification of tax cuts for the wealthy, and the "free to choose" mantra of Milton Friedman, who glorified "the power of the market" while elevating personal freedom to the first rank of capitalist virtues.

But what truly gave the animating spark to the idea of privatization was the stock market boom that began in the late 1980s. Lasting until the very eve of the twenty-first century, the bull market turned all America giddy with optimism about the riches to be made on Wall Street even by common folk. The country was seized with "irrational exuberance," as Federal Reserve chairman Alan Greenspan cautioned in 1996, when he thought the boom had already acquired a dangerous head of froth. He was correct, but his timing was slightly off. The bull still had three years to run.

Financial programs on television, with their scrolling stock tickers and toothy anchorpersons, aired nonstop not only in the high-tech trading rooms of financial firms but in barbershops and bars. A brace of new magazines popularized the once-occult art of stock picking, their headlines advising readers of "The 10 Stocks to Buy Now" or "The Best Investments for Your Retirement Future." Pundits assured a rapt audience that the market had crossed over to a "new paradigm," a permanent growth curve that would power the Dow Jones Industrial Average, then in the 11,000-point range, to 36,000 or higher. Any reversal was dismissed as merely a temporary dip and proclaimed a buying opportunity for anyone nimble enough to snap up bargains before the stampede resumed. For several years, the most exuberant forecasters were proven right again and again. The broad market yielded annual gains of more than 20 percent, and nobody thought the fun would ever end.

This was a dangerous period for the Social Security system. The rap that it was a bad financial deal for most workers never seemed truer than in the years when anybody's next-door neighbor might be making a killing in shares of Amazon and Yahoo. Privatization advocates wrote odes to the market's ability to turn even an average wage earner into a retirement millionaire via the inexorable appreciation of corporate stocks and the magic of compound interest.

"This isn't a game-show fantasy," gushed Sam Beard, a

former aide to Senator Robert F. Kennedy who had morphed into a self-styled capitalist (and who would later serve on President George W. Bush's privatization-happy 2001 Commission to Strengthen Social Security). "This isn't a lottery jackpot. This is a realistic goal." All that was required was for the average American to invest his or her payroll tax contributions in stocks, from which one would collect an annual return of 8 percent, a figure Beard characterized as a "prudent," even conservative, projection.

"When you retire, you'll be a millionaire," he wrote. "Whoever earns at least the minimum wage can become a millionaire in 45 years."

Beard's casual promise of millionairedom is a hallmark of privatization oratory as it was perfected during the roaring nineties. But he was only one voice in a mounting chorus. The Harvard economist Martin Feldstein, one of the gurus of privatization, seasoned his analytical tracts with dense computations comparing the rate of return achievable by private investments to the yield implicit in Social Security's tax and benefit formulas. The latter always came up dismally short, even accounting for the reality that privatization required individuals to make what Feldstein acknowledged were "risky investments."

But that risk was "market risk," which any investor could neutralize by purchasing professionally managed mutual funds. As a counterweight against what he regarded as the negligible chance that the impersonal capital markets might confound the predictions of experts, Feldstein pointed to the "risk" inherent in the Social Security system—the "political" risk that Congress might decide to cut benefits for hundreds of millions of Americans at some point in the future. For some reason he counted the latter hazard as the more perilous, notwithstanding the fact that since the founding of Social Security in 1935, Congress had never cut benefits for retirees. The stock market, by contrast, had suffered annual declines of more than 10 percent a dozen times since 1950 alone.

The main flaw in Feldstein's methodology soon became clear: contradicting the forecasts once again, the good times of the late 1990s didn't last. The stock market (as measured by Standard & Poor's benchmark 500 index) more than tripled in value from 1995 through 1999; but it fell 50 percent over the following four years. Investors who stood pat from 1995 through the end of 2003 would have seen two-thirds of their initial gains go up in smoke. If they were unfortunate enough to be entering retirement in 2003, their chances of recovering these losses would be effectively nil.

That unpredictability of market returns is one way that privatization undercuts one of the fundamental principles of Social Security, which is that even the meanest-paid worker deserves a reasonably secure and comfortable retirement. Private accounts would shift all the risk inherent in economic and market cycles onto the shoulders of people least able to bear it.

There is something perverse about the privatization doctrine's continued survival despite such powerful evidence of the stock market's willful volatility. In the mid-1930s, with the crash of 1929 still ringing in the nation's ears, Congress acknowledged the lesson by flatly forbidding the infant Social Security Administration to invest even a dime of its enrollees' hard-earned money in corporate stocks or bonds. In 2001, with the worst crash in three generations scarcely a year past, a presidential commission declared that the only way to save Social Security was for U. S. workers to turn over billions of dollars of their payroll contributions to those selfsame markets.

Although none of the major stock market indexes have come close (as of this writing) to recovering all the ground they lost in the most recent crash, privatization remains the centerpiece of numerous proposals to save Social Security. President Bush has even given the idea a fresh rhetorical flourish: private accounts are to be the cornerstone of an "ownership" society. Investors in these accounts will possess a hard asset that can't be taken from them by a spendthrift Congress, money they can pass on to their children and grandchildren (assuming they themselves don't outlive the cash).

Even more curiously, the recent history of the stock market hasn't stopped the privatization lobby from promising superior and safe investment returns to workers, if only they abandon Social Security entirely or in part. Shortly after helping the 2001 commission write its privatization proposals, Andrew Biggs, a functionary of the libertarian Cato Institute, showed that the privateers weren't so weak-kneed that they could be cowed by a mere market decline.

"Does a falling stock market mean the end of efforts to add personal accounts to Social Security?" he wrote. "It shouldn't." The march of the equity markets, he wrote confidently, guaranteed investors a healthy 7 percent annual return (cheating Beard's investors of a full percentage point). "Barring Armageddon, you can't lose."

It's worth noting that many economists doubt that the stock market's historical record of 7 to 8 percent annual postinflation appreciation over time can be sustained in the future. Some note that equity prices are still near a historical peak when reckoned in relation to corporate earnings. Others expect U.S. economic growth to slow significantly in coming decades. Among the pessimists are the Social Security trustees themselves, who have been projecting an annual economic growth rate of a mere 1.8 percent through 2080.

Because long-term stock market gains are closely tied to economic growth, many experts say that gains of over 7 percent a year are simply unachievable with a 1.8 percent economic growth rate; expert opinion is divided, but the consensus is that under those circumstances the more likely stock market return will be 3 to 4 percent annually. At that rate of return, many private account holders may well end up with smaller monthly retirement checks than they would receive from the existing Social Security system.

As a paradoxical aside, economists say that one condition that might produce stock market gains of more than 7 percent is an annual economic growth rate closer to the 3.3 percent experienced by the United States over the last 40 years. But if the economy does grow at such a clip, the Social Security trustees acknowledge, the system will remain financially healthy indefinitely, even without any increase in the payroll tax or any reduction in scheduled benefits.

In other words, if Social Security is in as bad a shape as privatization advocates claim, then private accounts can't produce the rich investment returns they promise. On the other hand, if the accounts can provide the forecasted gains, then Social Security is truly in fine shape. As the old phrase says, you pays your money and you takes your choice.

Of course, if it were really true that every investor, no matter what his or her wealth, contribution rate, age, and retirement date, could capture a steady 7 percent or 8 percent real portfolio return over 45 years, the world would truly be a paradise and we'd all be rich.

But with a few remarkable exceptions, even skilled professional investors generally fail to meet that standard—that's what gives the few investors who do succeed, like Warren Buffett and Peter Lynch, their mythical stature. Things don't happen that way in the real world of the investment markets, and not only because most people don't have billions of dollars to invest, as do Buffett and Lynch. So let's first examine the question: Why not?

The answer is bound up in the concept of risk.

Risk is perhaps the element of finance least understood by laypersons. Even when it's well understood, it's often ignored. (That's why the only people who consistently make money in casinos are the casino owners.) What most people know about risk can probably be summarized in the term "risk-reward ratio": To make a lot of money, you have to take a lot of risks.

The privatization lobby is extremely fond of citing the reward side of this equation—that's the side represented by the promise that private retirement accounts will turn us into a nation of millionaires. The promoters aren't so eager to publicize the other side of the deal, however, because if risk and reward are properly explained, many people will understand that the chance of doubling one's retirement nest egg may not be worth the concomitant chance of ending up with nothing.

It is generally true that risk pays greater rewards than safety and security. The investments that pay their holders the lowest yields are U.S. Treasury securities, which carry no risk premium thanks to the government's record of never having defaulted on its debt. This gilt-edged record explains why the government can pay relatively low interest rates on its securities and still have investors clamoring for more.

Because it's not as uncommon for corporations to default on their bonds, however, corporate bonds tend to carry higher interest rates than Treasuries. The few notches of additional interest assure investors that, at least as long as the company is functioning, they will receive higher quarterly payments to cover them against the mathematical chance that the company will stop paying altogether.

As a category, corporate equities are the riskiest financial investments. That's because if a company stumbles, its stockholders get squeezed most ruthlessly. In a bankruptcy, for instance, their holdings are almost always wiped out. (At least the bondholders often get to salvage a few pennies on the dollar.)

Stockholders are compensated for their risk by receiving the best overall rewards. If a company does well, the value of its shares rises not only with the improvement in its fortunes, but with the rosy expectations that other investors have for its future. By contrast, no matter how well a company is doing, its bond investors collect the interest rate denominated on its bonds, no more, no less. Their risk is less, but their upside is less, too.

Markets in risky securities tend to be jittery. The day-to-day price fluctuations of ultrasafe Treasury securities are almost infinitesimal. The prices of corporate bonds move more, but still fairly modestly, because the risk of a default is tempered by the steady stream of interest income paid while their issuers continue in business. But the price of a share of stock, as must be clear to anyone who has ever watched CNBC, is so closely tied to investors' expectations and fears that it can soar or collapse in a heartbeat.

The financial world knows of only two strategies to defeat risk. One is diversification: the more you spread your investments among different securities, the less the chance that the collapse of any single one of them will ruin you. The other is investing for the long term: taking the long view keeps you from buying or selling shares based on the fads and panics that sweep through the stock market almost daily.

Those are the circumstances under which risk can lead to reward. If you spread your investments widely and hang on for the long term, you can capture the higher yields of the broad stock market without suffering damage from the few companies that stumble, fall, or perish.

So now we know the source of the claim that, over the long term, stocks yield higher returns than bonds, especially government bonds. It's true—for the average broadly diversified investor hanging on for 20 years or more.

But we can't all be exactly average. How well does this work for the individual?

Unfortunately, not necessarily very well. Just because the broad market might return 8 percent annually over 30 years, it isn't true that *every* investor will earn the same 8 percent *every* year. Some might earn more, some much less.

This is important because some individual investors are less able to manage risk than others. A person on the eve of retirement is highly vulnerable to risk—he or she might have a large investment nest egg at peril and would have almost no time to earn back any losses. Younger workers are generally less vulnerable—they own less so they have less to lose, and they have more time to recover.

To see how this might work in an individual case, let's conjure up a worker named Rick Average. As his name implies, Rick earns an average wage all his working life. (The Social Security Administration pegged the average wage for 2004 at approximately $34,000.)

To simplify the math, let's say that, starting at age 20, Rick invests $1,000 a year in a private retirement account earning 8 percent. When he's ready to retire at 65, his account will hold approximately $386,000. Or rather, that is what it would hold if it invariably earned the *average* long-term 8 percent annual yield every year.

But that's not how the markets work in the real world. Rick's portfolio is just one data point in a nationwide—indeed, a world-wide—aggregate. The average of the returns experienced by all stock investors over the entire 45-year period may be 8 percent, but any given portfolio might earn more or less than that—might even go negative—in any given year. So we see that one fallacy buried in the privateers' rate-of-return promises is that the average rate earned by all owners of private accounts is *equivalent* to the rate earned by each of the owners. There's only one way for that to be true: pool all the owners' accounts in one fund, and dole it out equally. As it happens, that resembles how traditional Social Security works.

The privateers are fond of making sweeping claims: for example, they say that there's never been a 45-year stretch in which stock investors have lost money; in effect, they're saying that the volatile short-term swings of the investment markets are completely leveled out over the long term, and therefore that all workers who rely on the investment markets will retire with roughly equivalent investment gains.

But the truth is that there has been great variability in investment returns over successive 45-year stretches. If we look at annual returns over 20 successive periods, starting with the period 1950–1994 and ending with 1969–2003, we find that the average annual return ranged from a high of 8.64 percent (1954–1998) to a low of 6.33 percent (1959–2003). Investment portfolios held during these time frames would vary widely in value. The average 20-year-old worker who invested $1,000 in the stock market every year starting in 1954 would have about $470,000 at the end of the 45-year time frame in 1998. The worker who started in 1959, however, would end up with $234,000—half as much—at the end of his or her 45-year block in 2003, despite having invested exactly the same sum for the same number of years.

This variability isn't a very critical issue if we're talking about supplemental retirement investments, such as 401(k) plans or IRA accounts. Those are voluntary programs, after all, and any gain over inflation should be regarded as a plus.

But it's a much bigger deal if the accounts are expected to provide basic retirement funds and are accumulated from compulsory taxes, as Social Security accounts would be. In that case, the disparity in resources of different retirement cohorts could have severe social and political repercussions.

Those lucky enough to win what the economist Christian E. Weller calls the "generational lottery"—workers who happened to retire in the midst of the 1990s bull market, for example— would end up with far healthier pensions than those who drew the bum ticket—say, those whose retirement dates fell immediately after the bubble burst. A wide fluctuation in the fortunes of retirees based on market conditions is incompatible with the Social Security principle that the risks of retirement should be spread across generations.

As the economists Peter A. Diamond and Peter R. Orszag observe, private accounts don't provide much capacity for extending a hand across the generations. "Political pressure might be brought to bear to bail out cohorts who have had unfortunate experiences under an individual accounts system," they say, but there's no certainty that the pressure would work. Indeed, they believe it is "not likely that cohorts with unusually high returns will be forced to help later, less fortunate cohorts."

That said, a sharp decline in retiree wealth might lead to economic problems too great for the government to ignore. Older persons might decide to work longer instead of retiring; this could lead to higher unemployment among the young. With poor returns affecting an entire generation, not merely a few unfortunate or unwise investors, lawmakers might have no choice but to bail out the system. And that would eradicate the budget gains that will supposedly be derived from Social Security.

Stock market volatility doesn't only affect investors' returns; it also destroys the predictability of retiree resources. This is a more important factor in retirement than might be evident at first glance. Those who are dependent on investment returns, as many would be under a system of private accounts, might be misled by a string of good annual returns into making retirement decisions that could be undercut by a sudden market reversal. That's because the pattern of gains and losses in the market over even the short term has a strong effect on the judgments we make about our wealth.

Remember Rick Average, who expected to earn 8 percent annually on the private account to which he contributed $1,000 a year? Even if his gains and losses average out to 8 percent over his lifetime, his returns in individual years will vary widely. In some years he'll earn 25 percent, in others 4 percent, in still others he may even *lose* 25 percent. But the impact of a 25 percent loss on Rick's retirement planning will vary significantly based on when it occurs in his career.

Let's say it strikes the year after he opens his account, when his portfolio amounts to only $1,000. The hit reduces his nest egg to $750. But he still has 44 years of deposits and investment returns ahead of him, so the long-term impact is muted.

But what if the crash occurs in year 45? At that point, Rick's holdings will have grown to more than $386,000. A 25 percent drop in the stock market will cost him roughly $100,000 on the spot.

One can argue that the remaining $286,000 is still a tidy sum. If Rick had kept his expectations in check over his lifetime he need not have been unpleasantly surprised at the occasional sudden loss. But while the hypothetical individuals who populate economists' models behave unemotionally, human beings don't. As he approached his retirement date, Rick is likely to have based a considerable amount of planning on the expectation of entering his golden years with a $386,000 cushion. He might have factored in the higher sum when he calculated his annuity, bought a retirement home, or scheduled his last day of work. If the market shreds those plans, what are his options?

He might be able to recover some losses by deferring his retirement for a couple of years, assuming he has other resources to live on or the opportunity to continue working. People who delayed retiring from 2002 until late in 2004, for example, were able to recover more than a third of the losses they had suffered in the prior market downturn.

But considering that two-thirds of Americans 65 and older depend on Social Security for the majority of their income, it's plain that most workers nearing retirement don't have that flexibility. "Few can control the timing of their retirement," observes the Boston College retirement expert Alicia Munnell. "Thus, most future beneficiaries are not in a position to take a gamble" on private accounts.

The impact of sudden investment losses late in life explains why financial planners generally advise their clients to move gradually out of stocks and into bond investments or even cash equivalents as retirement draws near. But shifting into safer investments means accepting lower average returns than those of stocks. At the end of 2004, U.S. Treasury bonds were yielding 3.5 percent to 4 percent, and money market funds—the most common proxies for cash—returned less than 2 percent. Those low yields don't mean one should avoid such investments, but they do explain why forecasts of a steady annual appreciation of 8 percent for private accounts are unrealistic.

Professional economists, who understand that risk carries a cost, go to great lengths to compensate for it in measuring the relative value of alternative investments over the long term. To accommodate the reality that higher yields always involve higher uncertainty, they use risk-adjusted returns, meaning that they ignore the higher average returns of riskier investments such as stocks, and base their forecasts on the prevailing interest rates on U.S. Treasury bonds, the safest investments.

The U.S. government itself uses risk-adjusted returns in forecasting investment growth in the portfolios it controls, including those of the Railroad Retirement System, a special federal pension plan. Federal law, in fact, forbids corporate pension plans to use projected stock market returns in estimating their own future assets. As for the Social Security system, it owns only Treasury securities, so risk-adjusted returns are built into its forecasts.

But promoters of privatization fling around projections unadjusted for risk with abandon. In early 2005, the Cato Institute posted on its website a "Social Security Benefit Calculator," enabling users to calculate their future private account values, assuming they invested their 6.2 percent payroll tax in a portfolio partially comprising stocks returning 7 percent annually over inflation. The calculator gratifyingly showed that most workers would reach retirement with astounding wealth. The only thing missing was a guarantee that the real world would cooperate.

> I particularly like the idea of a Social Security system that recognizes the importance and value of ownership. People who own something have a stake in the future of their country and they have a vital interest in the policies of their government.
> —GEORGE W. BUSH, December 16, 2004

The Bush doctrine of ownership, as applied to Social Security, rests on two slogans: "It's my money" and "Who can manage it better than myself?" At the January 11 dog-and-pony show with which we opened this book, President Bush neatly packaged them together this way: "I've heard some say, well, this is risky, to allow people to invest their own money. But it's *not* risky."

The notion that one should have complete freedom to invest—and spend—one's own retirement nest egg certainly has strong appeal. However—and here we risk saying something quite unfashionable, not to say mildly insulting—it's not applicable to the Social Security system.

Let's consider the two elements of the ownership doctrine separately. First, is the money in Social Security really "my money"?

The answer is no, in the same sense that my income tax, once forked over to the Internal Revenue Service, is no longer "my" money. It henceforth belongs to the national Treasury, to be spent at the discretion of the White House and Congress on federal programs. These include some programs I may not personally endorse and others I might like to endow with an even greater proportion of my largesse. The law states that I have no right to pick and choose which programs are financed by my income taxes (except for a presidential campaign fund to which I may direct $3 a year by checking a box on my Form 1040). Numerous so-called tax protesters have faced jail and a stiff fine for leading credulous taxpayers to believe otherwise.

Social Security seems different on the surface, partially because of Franklin Roosevelt's decision in 1935 to label payroll tax levies "contributions" to the program. As we have seen, FDR had some sound reasons for foisting this nomenclature on the public. He hoped that a metaphor drawn from the world of insurance would sustain public support for the program and discourage congressional tampering. He also thought that the notion of Social Security as a return of workers' own capital would distinguish it from a welfare handout, the detested "dole."

This theoretical linkage between contributions and benefits encourages people to imagine that their payroll taxes go into a sort of safe-deposit box with their name inscribed on the outside. It is true that the greater one's earnings, the larger one's monthly stipend. The connection is far from exact, however; it's "quite loose, and quite mysterious," as the Nobel Prize–winning economist James Tobin has observed. While higher-earning workers do receive larger monthly Social Security checks in absolute dollars, lower-earning workers receive more in relative terms, as their initial Social Security checks are equivalent to a larger percentage of their final years' wages.

FDR's terminology and the peculiarities of the benefit formula have bequeathed us 70 years of misunderstanding, but the fact remains that individuals no more have a direct claim on their payroll tax contributions than they do on their income tax payments. Once a Social Securtiy deduction is taken from a paycheck, it belongs to the program, not the individual.

That makes good sense for several reasons. One is the pay-as-you-go structure established for Social Security in 1935, in which every working generation's taxes pay for the benefits of current retirees. This arrangement would be impossible if every worker owned a direct claim on the fruits of his or her contributions.

The pooling of payroll taxes is also what makes possible Social Security's most salient social insurance features. These include enhanced stipends for lower-earning retirees and disability coverage for those who become injured before they can contribute a lifetime share to the system. It allows dependent benefits to be paid to children who have never contributed a dime in payroll tax, and survivor benefits to be paid to spouses who may have given up their own jobs to raise children or assist in their partners' careers. It funds the guaranteed monthly benefits paid to retirees in their eighties and nineties by, in effect, subsidizing them from the taxes paid by workers who die in their fifties and sixties.

Obviously, these provisions all create winners and losers. But the rationale for Social Security's insurance component is that no one can be sure in advance into which of these groups—the advantaged or disadvantaged—one will fall during a lifetime.

Diverting revenues from the system to individual accounts would cripple Social Security's ability to assist retirees, the disabled, and dependents whose needs exceed their contributions. Trying to maintain the system's social insurance goals while funding private accounts from today's level of payroll taxes would place the system, or the federal budget, under enormous financial strain.

What of the second tenet of the ownership doctrine—that everyone knows best how to invest his or her money?

This idea presupposes that every investor has an equal chance of capturing the greatest possible return on his or her money—in other words, that the likelihood that anyone will make an imprudent or unlucky choice, or even be defrauded, is insignificant. It further supposes that the owners of private retirement accounts will invariably select the optimum mix of investments for themselves. In sum, it is based on the theory that all investors have equivalent knowledge about the investment market and equivalent skills in exploiting it.

Milton Friedman, the prophet of modern laissez-faire economics and a founding philosopher of the privatization school, is one of those who vests an almost mystical faith in the flawless decision-making capacity of today's workers. "Our general presumption," he writes, "is that individuals can best judge for themselves how to use their resources."

In real life, unfortunately, even professionals make billion-dollar investment blunders. Laymen, who tend to be crammed into the caboose of the information train that serves Wall Street, are easily led, even misled. Indeed, one tenet of professional investing is that when small investors pile into the stock market, the time is ripe for the pros to get out.

Government regulators have always worried about the pitfalls facing inexperienced workers trying to invest for their retirements. As Arthur Levitt, then the chairman of the Securities and Exchange Commission, cautioned in 1998, uninformed investors "risk making poor investment decisions—perhaps even because they fell prey to fraudulent advice or misleading sales practices." Giving the average person too many choices for how to invest money without providing adequate investor education and rigorously policing the investment industry, Levitt said, "will provide the unscrupulous with new opportunities to deceive and distort."

Many retirement experts and economists say that an often-overlooked virtue of Social Security is that, as a compulsory defined-benefit program, it removes choice and decision-making from the process of saving for retirement. That it's difficult to persuade many workers, especially the young, of the need to prepare for an event that might be four decades away is an article of faith among retirement consultants. As Tobin writes, many workers "who think they could provide better for their own retirement than by contributing to [Social Security], would in fact not succeed in doing so." He adds, in a wicked gibe at Friedman and his advocacy for making Social Security voluntarily, "Many would not in fact save the equivalent of their payroll taxes if they were free to choose."

Privateers disdain such views as paternalistic or elitist. The president, striking a populist pose, remarked at his January 11 session: "There's kind of an assumption that only a certain group of people at a certain income can manage an account. It's as if you've got to have a net worth of 'X' before savings becomes a real part of your life. I reject that."

It turns out that the United States has been running a sort of laboratory experiment in the investing behavior of regular workers for more than a quarter-century, and the results have proven Bush wrong.

The laboratory is the 401(k) plan, which was created in 1978 to allow workers to build tax-deferred retirement accounts by investing a percentage of their annual pay, some of which may be matched by employers, in stocks, bonds, and mutual funds.

The plans have manifold virtues, which is why they've attracted $1.9 trillion in contributions from 42 million workers. Employers often match as much as 50 percent of their employees' contributions. The plans provide a rare tax shelter for middle-income savers. But there are also troubling signs that instructing workers how to make prudent investments based on their own circumstances and needs has been harder than anyone expected.

Several studies suggest that the greater the number of investment options presented to plan enrollees, the greater the chance that they will choose the wrong ones for their personal circumstances. The Employee Benefit Research Institute, a nonprofit group backed by large corporations and employee benefit firms, has found that many workers make rudimentary blunders in asset allocation—that is, in apportioning their assets among the various choices.

Although younger people should have the largest allocation of stocks in their portfolios because they are best positioned to bear the risks of the equity market, EBRI found that 60 percent of all workers in their twenties kept less than half of their assets in stock mutual funds. Some 38 percent had no equities in their portfolios at all. At the other end of the age spectrum, 13 percent of workers in their sixties, and therefore on the eve of retirement, still had more than 90 percent of their portfolios in stocks—an allocation many experts would consider excessively risky.

Employees tended to invest too much money in their own companies' shares, which is inadvisable because it magnifies their exposure to any problems that may arise at those companies. And they weren't very nimble in reacting to the volatility of the stock market; relatively few had made any allocation changes in their funds in the wake of the recent market crash.

In general, the performance of self-managed 401(k) plans has trailed that of traditional professionally managed pension plans. Between 1986 and 2000, traditional plans gained an average 7.9 percent a year, while 401(k) plans earned 7.1 percent. That's a big gap: Over 45 years, the difference in the final value of a $10,000 initial investment would be nearly $100,000.

Privatization advocates contend that workers are clamoring for more personal flexibility in their retirement investment decisions, but the evidence is equivocal. "It's not at all clear to me that people want this responsibility," says Alicia Munnell. "Many don't really enjoy investing on their own."

Munnell's own studies indicate that about 25 percent of all eligible workers don't participate in 401(k) plans, and fewer than 10 percent contribute the maximum allowed. One reason may be that some workers don't have spare cash to set aside for a voluntary retirement fund. But it may also be true that the complexity of investing and the heavy responsibility of managing one's own retirement kitty turns people off. As the Chicago labor lawyer and author Thomas Geoghegan put it in a witty column: "In real life, we ignore our Social Security. That's the glory of it . . . I've already got enough to do."

Defenders of privatization say there's a convenient way to discourage workers from making poor investment decisions like misallocating assets or punting their money on a fad stock due to collapse, like Krispy Kreme or Pets.com. They would limit private retirement investments to a tightly regulated set of mutual funds carefully designed to track the broad stock and bond markets.

While that might work in theory, it plainly runs counter to the very notion of ownership, which presumably confers the right to do what one wishes with one's own assets. Such restrictions may also run into opposition from the financial services industry, which collects higher fees from selling more complex investment programs (much as the auto industry collects larger profit margins on SUVs than on two-door coupes). Wall Street may not be contented with the slender profits to be made from selling plain-vanilla mutual funds. Indeed, the trend in 401(k) plans, most of which are managed by large commercial brokerage firms, is a move toward more choices, not fewer—the average large plan now offers 38 investment options, up from 14 in 1995.

That brings us to the inherent contradiction of restricting the investment options and withdrawal rights of an "ownership" account. Here, too, the government has been running a laboratory—the Individual Retirement Account, or IRA, created by Congress in 1982 to allow people to deposit savings of up to $2,000 a year in tax-deferred accounts.

IRA rules originally imposed a heavy penalty of 10 percent and a high income tax rate on any money withdrawn before an account owner reached the age of 59½. But public pressure gradually forced Congress to ease the withdrawal restrictions. At first, owners were permitted to use IRA funds to cover medical expenses. A few years later, an exemption was added for the purchase of a first home. Eventually the exemption was expanded further to cover college or graduate school tuition.

Could Congress resist similar political pressure from Social Security plan "owners"? It's doubtful. But even devoted privateers acknowledge that there will be unhappy consequences if lawmakers cave in: millions of people might reach retirement age with their nest eggs vacuumed clean. "If that were to happen, the same people would almost certainly appear hat in hand on the steps of Congress, expecting to be bailed out of their plight," observes Sylvester Schieber, a member of the 1994 Social Security advisory council. The Social Security system would be back where it started.

Let's now consider one other selling point of private accounts—that they are assets that can be bequeathed to an owner's heirs.

Once again, President Bush is his own most exuberent salesman: "Owning your own personal savings account," he says, "allows you to pass on your savings to whoever you choose. You can't do that in Social Security today."

As with most privatization sales pitches, this promise comes accompanied by several columns of small print. In financial terms, there is an inherent incompatibility in an account that can supposedly provide for your own secure retirement *and* be passed on to your survivors. To put it another way, moving an asset from one generation to the next is a zero-sum transaction—the more you bequeath, the less you can keep for your own purposes. In intergenerational finance, as in most things, there is no such thing as a free lunch.

Social Security pays heed to this rule by limiting the money that can be paid to a worker's survivors. A deceased retiree's spouse generally receives 100 percent of the worker's retirement benefit until he or she dies; dependent children receive a stipend of their own until they turn 18 (or 19, if they are enrolled in primary or secondary school). But there is no provision for paying benefits to adult children, much less to grandchildren, great-grandchildren, or later generations. (In certain circumstances, such as when a beneficiary is caring for grandchildren whose parents are deceased or disabled, the grandchildren can receive survivor benefits.) This is one way that Social Security conserves its resources so it has enough to cover the present generation's needs.

Indeed, it would be almost impossible to fashion a system of private accounts that guaranteed a comfortable retirement for their owners under all circumstances and also guaranteed a substantial share for heirs. Here's why.

Start with the proposition that society has an interest in ensuring that owners of private accounts don't outlive their assets. If they run out of money during their lifetime, after all, society will end up footing the bill for their sustenance—the very outcome that Social Security aims to prevent. The only way to ensure a lifetime benefit is to require that every owner of a private account convert it into an annuity—a guaranteed lifetime stream of monthly payments—upon retirement.

Mandatory annuitization is a thorny issue for the privatization lobby. The conversion always comes at a price, because it's essentially a statistical gamble. An annuity company—usually an insurance firm, bank, or brokerage—accepts a lump sum from an investor and commits to pay him or her a monthly check for life in return. The company has to estimate how long the recipient might live, using statistical tables based on ethnic and racial background, income, health, and even place of residence. It also projects its own investment yield on the lump sum. Using these two factors, it calculates a payout for the customer that will also produce a reasonable profit for itself. The company assumes the risk that customers will live, and therefore collect checks, longer than it projects; customers gamble that they will live so long that their total payments will at least equal the value of their deposit, plus the interest it would have earned, over their remaining years.

The longer an annuity company expects the customer to live, and the lower the prevailing interest rate at the time of conversion, the lower the guaranteed monthly payment offered the customer. Some companies also charge a separate conversion fee. Because annuity buyers today tend to be well-heeled individuals who have led comfortable lives and taken care of themselves, and therefore have fairly long life expectancies at retirement, annuity companies tend to charge very steep fees; some estimates place the cost of conversion at as much as 20 percent of the original asset value.

No one knows what would happen to average costs if the annuity market were spread over all retirees, as it would be if private accounts were broadly implemented. Theoretically, the average fees for annuities would fall, but the theory has never been tested. All that can be said for sure is that annuity fees are a hidden cost of private accounts, rarely mentioned by privatization supporters.

What is known, however, is that annuity payouts are highly sensitive to the prevailing interest rate at the moment of conversion; the higher the rate, the better the deal. Using standard financial formulas and ignoring transaction fees and brokerage profits, a $100,000 account converted when prevailing interest rates were 7 percent would produce an annuity of $10,000 a year for 18 years, the current average life expectancy of an American white male at 65. With interest rates at 4 percent, the same $100,000 lump sum would yield only $7,900 a year.

This raises the prospect that different cohorts might fare very differently in the annuity market, an effect similar to the one created by fluctuations in the stock market.

It should be obvious that mandatory annuitization is incompatible with passing money on to later generations; when an annuity holder dies, the annuity dies, too. For that reason, mandatory annuitization might be a hard sell as part of the privatization of Social Security. Indeed, few proposals for private accounts anticipate such a requirement. Certainly it can't be part of any Bush administration plan based on the ability to pass money on to heirs.

Yet, allowing owners of private retirement accounts complete freedom to decide how and when to spend their money risks throwing the Social Security system severely out of balance. For all that President Bush assures us that no administration plan would allow retirees to blow their entire accounts in Las Vegas, it would be administratively and politically difficult to craft a formula that allowed certain kinds of spending but not others. As even fans of private accounts acknowledge, there would be little to prevent some retirees from deliberately overspending their accounts in the expectation that, if worse comes to worst, they will still qualify for welfare (a phenomenon known as "moral hazard").

Nor can there be any guarantee that even frugal and responsible retirees might not simply miscalculate, outliving even the most carefully judged daily expenditures and becoming public wards despite their best-laid plans.

Any of these outcomes underscores an important drawback of private retirement accounts: they would undermine Social Security's basic purpose of providing benefits that last to the end of the beneficiary's life.

But that's not where the downside of privatization ends. It not only introduces risk and complexity into all workers' planning for retirement; it introduces enormous costs, too.

Chapter Ten

The Ownership Scam 2: Costs or Benefits?

F RANCIS X. CAVANAUGH had a succinct opinion of the prospects for creating cost-effective private retirement accounts within the Social Security system:

"Impossible."

That's what he told the House Ways and Means Committee in 1998, when it was pondering the feasibility of setting up private accounts styled after the federal Thrift Savings Plan, a pension fund for government employees. The TSP at the time managed $100 million in stock and bond investments for 2.9 million members. Then, as now, it was a model for what the privatization lobby wanted to create as a replacement for Social Security.

The committee members couldn't have found a better-informed expert. As the first executive director and chief executive officer of the Federal Retirement Thrift Investment Board, Cavanaugh had created the TSP in 1986. He continued running it until 1994, when he went into the private consulting business. Nothing he has heard since then has dissuaded him from thinking that a system of private retirement accounts cannot possibly be run as efficiently as a centralized defined-contribution fund like the TSP.

He has pointed out that the sheer number of such accounts would be enormous and the average balance relatively tiny. Administrative fees would eat deeply into the account assets during their first few years, leaving account holders with rates of return so meager that their earnings might never catch up to what they would collect from traditional Social Security. The Social Security Administration would face huge costs of its own, stemming from the unprecedented administrative burdens imposed by private accounts. Small businesses would be overwhelmed by the paperwork necessary to track their employees' contributions.

And those are only the costs he could foresee. "This is unknown territory," he told the congressional committee. All that is known for sure is that everyone who has tried to create a private retirement program with individual accounts as small as those in a privatized Social Security system has failed, because the goals and characteristics of a social insurance program and a private pension plan are fundamentally at odds. Combining the features of the TSP with those of Social Security, he says, would be "like mating a bear with a bee—somebody is going to get hurt."

The privateers have tuned him out. President Bush's handpicked 2001 Social Security reform commission fashioned its privatization model on the TSP, and the White House still makes the same pitch. In his 2005 State of the Union address, President Bush evoked the Thrift Savings Plan in describing what he planned to do to Social Security. "Personal retirement accounts should be familiar to federal employees, because you already have something similar," he said. "It's time to extend the same security, and choice, and ownership to young Americans. . . ."

The unique complexities and costs of converting Social Security to a private system have always been among the privateers' dirty little secrets. Social Security is the federal government's most cost-effective program, a model for public social-insurance systems around the world. Even a partial transition to private accounts would make that distinction a thing of the past.

The shift would likely raise administrative costs 10- or 15-fold, require expanding the Social Security Administration workforce by as many as 100,000 new employees—more than doubling its size—and require either trillions of dollars in cash transfers from the federal budget or an equivalent increase in the national debt. But while privatization advocates occasionally acknowledge that such costs may loom on the horizon, they hastily redefine them away as "investments in the future of Social Security" or "prepayments" of the system's long-term deficit. These arguments are attempts to gloss over the truth, which is that the conversion would require taking trillions of dollars from benefits, government programs, or taxpayers.

Ironically, this expensive conversion won't accomplish what President Bush claims to be his primary goal—to make Social Security fiscally more robust. Even the White House's top advisers admit that privatization won't improve the system's financial condition, and may indeed worsen it over the next four to six decades.

Transition costs are a dangerous topic for the privateers, not only because of their size in purely monetary terms, but because changing Social Security to a private investment program will be an unpredictably complicated operation.

Cavanaugh is not the only pension expert to recognize this. John Kimpel, a senior executive at Fidelity Investments, has observed, "No existing system is sufficient to take on this enormous task." He noted that, although the country has had extensive experience with defined contribution programs such as the TSP, 401(k) plans, and individual retirement accounts, none could serve the entire national workforce, as Social Security does, without "substantial cost."

The conversion costs fall into two main categories. The first is administrative.

Employer-sponsored programs such as the TSP and 401(k) plans require central record keeping on a scale usually manageable only by large enterprises, such as major corporations or federal agencies. That's because the contributions deducted from employees' paychecks must be carefully allocated to the investment pools the employees select. The programs place other labor-intensive demands on their sponsors, including the distribution of forms and notices and scheduling educational sessions for enrollees. None of these tasks is required for Social Security.

These requirements drive the cost of the TSP's central administration to an average of about $25 per participant a year. That's more than twice the administrative cost of Social Security, but it's still low compared to the costs of most private pension plans.

Even so, that figure may be misleading. One rarely mentioned factor in the TSP's vaunted efficiency is its ability to shift many of its administrative chores to the federal agencies that employ its members. A large share of the system's costs, accordingly, is submerged in the agencies' budgets. The agencies' payroll departments are in charge of making timely and accurate deposits to individuals' accounts, and their human-resources departments handle enrollment formalities and investor education.

The TSP can't even say how much in expenses it sheds in this manner: Asked by the president's 2001 Social Security commission if he knew how much in expenses the TSP offloaded to its member federal agencies, the thrift program's chief at the time, Roger Mehle, said he had absolutely no idea. "We don't see them," he said.

Another factor helping to keep TSP costs low is that its members are relatively well-paid and their accounts relatively sizable. The average TSP member's annual contribution is $4,200 and the average account balance is $34,000. This is important because the cost of servicing a small account is about the same as a large one, so small investment accounts are likely to become overburdened by costs that large accounts can absorb more easily.

The average Social Security private account wouldn't approach the size of a TSP account. Consider the Bush commission's proposal that workers be permitted to deposit up to 4 percentage points of their annual wages, or a maximum of $1,000 a year, in private accounts. Even granting the most optimistic investment return projected by private account advocates—say, 8 percent a year—an account funded with the maximum contribution would need more than 17 years to match the $34,000 average balance in the TSP. Most workers would be investing much less than the maximum $1,000 a year, so their accounts would grow even more slowly.

Assuming that two-thirds of all Social Security recipients opened private accounts (a common projection of the accounts' acceptance rate), privatization would produce nearly 100 million small accounts, each incurring fairly high fixed costs. How high? Estimates of administrative fees for 401(k) plans, many of which include much smaller accounts than the TSP average, vary widely, but even the low end is more than five times higher than Social Security's administrative cost. It's important to understand, furthermore, that unlike Social Security, which absorbs administrative costs centrally, the costs of defined contribution programs like the TSP and 401(k) plans are paid by the participating workers. The effect of even a nominal fee can be significant over time. An annual charge of 1 percent of assets, for instance, would reduce an investment account's balance by more than 20 percent after 40 years.

Moreover, there are no assurances that the fees charged to owners of private retirement accounts would be standardized at 1 percent. It's possible that investment firms managing private accounts would insist on recovering a larger share of their own costs from participants. Cavanaugh has estimated that in the first years of a privatized system administration fees could amount to 3 percent or more of workers' balances. That's roughly the equivalent of the after-tax yield on an account invested in risk-free securities such as Treasury bonds; in other words, the administrative costs of private accounts could wipe out the investment gains of all but the most aggressive investors. Cavanaugh contends that under those circumstances, most accounts are likely to lose money for years.

Workers would also bear the costs of administrative snafus, which may be numerous in the first years of such a novel and intricate retirement system. If contributions go astray in a traditional defined-benefit program such as Social Security, it's the system that incurs the loss, not the member—the program must pay the beneficiary an amount set by formula regardless of whether it has properly recorded every contribution. If money in defined-contribution plans goes astray, however, it's the plan's owners who lose.

The administrative requirements of private accounts would fall most heavily on small businesses, which have little experience with pension plans in which employee contributions must be handled promptly and meticulously. Such care costs money. Financial-services firms that provide record keeping and investment services to employers usually don't even recommend that small businesses sponsor 401(k) plans, because the costs of running such plans need to be spread over scores or hundreds of accounts. Kimpel's firm, Fidelity Investments, generally doesn't advise employers with fewer than 25 workers to offer 401(k) plans. As a result, the more than two-thirds of all businesses in the United States with fewer than ten employees remain "outside the scope of the 401(k) industry," as Cavanaugh observes.

Even large sponsors can fall prey to administrative disaster. Consider what happened when the TSP tried to build a new record-keeping system in 1996. When its contractor failed to get the system operational after four years of trying, the TSP fired the firm, squandering more than $36 million of members' funds in the process. A new contractor finally completed the system in 2003—after spending an additional $32 million.

The Social Security Administration itself isn't currently geared up to handle the most critical aspect of moving money into individual accounts—depositing the funds promptly—and it may not be able to do so without fundamentally changing how the payroll tax is collected and recorded.

Because Social Security is, in effect, one big tureen from which all benefit payments are ladled out, the timing of deposits doesn't matter to individual workers. Although employers must regularly transfer payroll withholdings to the government (usually quarterly), they're not required to deliver a detailed accounting of how much came from each particular worker's paycheck until the February following the end of every calendar year. The Social Security Administration then spends another seven months reconciling the data on its own books. In other words, although the government receives employee contributions often within weeks of their being deducted from paychecks, the lag time before it matches the deductions to the contributors can be as long as 19 months (the average is about nine months). Applying such a delay to private accounts would mean that the average employee contribution would be left fallow, earning virtually no investment return, for the better part of a year.

It would hardly suit the owners of individual accounts for their investment choices to remain unfulfilled for such a long period. They might find themselves watching impotently as market rallies took off while their cash remained on the sidelines. Or they might be provoked by a market crash into feverish attempts to reverse their investment choices, hoping to salvage whatever money hasn't yet been allocated—thus creating further administrative confusion for the system. No one has yet proposed a simple way of reconciling the dawdling habits of the Social Security Administration to the rapid pace of events in the investment markets.

The TSP and 401(k) sponsors provide many other administrative services that the Social Security Administration would be hard-pressed to match for private account owners. It's a rare defined-contribution program today that doesn't offer 24-hour toll-free telephone service and websites to handle withdrawals and investment orders, deliver daily updates of account balances, and answer enrollees' questions. Fidelity performed 450 million financial transactions for its 5 million 401(k) clients in

2003; how many transactions would be required by a system composed of 50 million or more Social Security accounts? Kimpel's back-of-the-envelope estimate was that the Social Security Administration would need at least three years to build an adequate service system, and that as many as 100,000 new employees would be needed to run it.

The only way Social Security might be able to avoid the burden, Kimpel suggested, would be to limit the services it provides to participants. This could mean keeping workers' investment options very narrow, restricting their right to change investment choices, say, to once or twice a year—and dispensing with such common customer perks as daily or weekly account updates. Would these restrictions be regarded by individual account holders as consistent with "ownership"? In the uncharted territory of privatized Social Security, no one can guess. But the chances are that the servicing of Social Security private accounts would not match what is provided by the Thrift Savings Plan or 401(k)s.

The second category of transition costs is connected with Social Security's cash flow. Under the system's pay-as-you-go structure, as we have noted, money collected from today's workers as payroll tax is disbursed to pay benefits to today's retirees.*

Under the principle proposal of President Bush's 2001 reform commission, a worker could choose to divert up to 4 percentage points of his or her payroll tax—or almost one-third of the 12.4

---

*To be precise, a true one-to-one correspondence doesn't exist at the moment. As a consequence of the 1983 amendments, the payroll tax produces roughly 11 percent more revenue than the system needs each year, with the surplus paid into the trust fund. But the principle is still valid.

percent tax shared between employee and employer—into an individual account, rather than leaving it in the pool used to pay benefits. What would happen to the system's balance sheet if all workers chose this option?

Let's say the option were implemented starting in 2008. Judging from the system's own intermediate-case projections, the tax diversion would place Social Security nearly $120 billion in the hole in the very first year: while its benefit and administrative costs would be fixed at approximately $590 billion, its revenues from the payroll tax and income taxes charged on benefits would drop from $702 billion to $472 billion. By 2013 the cumulative deficit would approach $1 trillion, and by shortly after 2020 the red ink would reach $2 trillion.

The commission's plan, like other typical privatization proposals, would compensate for the lost resources by offsetting a worker's diversion of his or her payroll tax by a commensurate reduction of benefits at retirement. The commission recommended a formula under which a worker who diverted 4 percent of his pay, or one-third of his payroll tax, would have his basic retirement stipend cut by one-third, compounded at inflation plus 2 percent a year. As long as the worker's private account earned more than 2 percent over inflation, therefore, he or she would receive more from combining a Social Security check and the balance in his or her private account than from staying entirely within Social Security.

The problem is that these offsets would relieve the system's cash-flow problem only after a delay of several decades. That's because revenue loss would start to mount as soon as workers set up private accounts, but the recovery through offsetting benefits wouldn't kick in until the workers retired and received reduced benefits. The delay could be as long as 45 years.

That explains why critics say, and many supporters agree, that private accounts by themselves will diminish Social Security's financial stability for many decades to come. It's also why most privatization plans rely on dramatic benefit reductions *in addition to* the offsets in order to "save" the system from bankruptcy.

Of course, benefits would still have to be paid to retirees, disabled workers, and family members while money was leaching out of the system into private accounts. Where would the necessary funds come from? During the late 1990s, privatization gurus had an easy answer: from the federal budget surplus, which reached $230 billion in the last year of the Clinton administration and was projected to rise to a total of $5 trillion over the following decade.

The Clinton surplus had the privateers licking their chops. The Cato Institute placed transition funding foremost on its list of priorities for spending the money—even ahead of general income tax relief. A mere $4 trillion in transferred surplus money, the libertarian think tank calculated, could finance a diversion of 8 percent of payroll into private accounts, quadrupling the size of the accounts it had previously proposed

As things developed, of course, the surplus evaporated before any such program could be put in place—converted into a record deficit in the first years of the Bush administration, not by the needs of Social Security but by two wars and a string of income tax cuts.

Bereft of cash for the transition, the privateers changed their tune. Henceforth, the party line was that there had never been such a thing as transition costs in the first place. The money spent in the first decades of the transition would only be temporary red ink, because it would relieve society of the costly burden of Social Security later on. If one were to take a sufficiently long view, the whole process would be a wash. In the words of economist Martin Feldstein, the deficits of the early transition years would be "really a down payment on lower taxes down the line." It would be improper to treat them as "traditional" deficits at all, he explained, because the borrowed money would be transferred directly to citizens to save and invest, with the gains to be repaid in the future.

The shortcoming of this argument is that government deficits are almost always rationalized as investments in the future. Debt is incurred to build infrastructure, such as highways and bridges, which presumably produce long-term economic benefits; or to stimulate economic growth in a battle against recession or depression; or even to finance short-term needs without imposing the dead weight of high taxes on wealthy citizens, who will deploy their retained wealth in wise and virtuous projects that will profit themselves and society at large. In each case, government borrowings crowd out private investment and raise government costs as long as the debt remains outstanding.

Would the international finance markets perceive that the deficits incurred to finance a transition to private accounts are more salubrious than any other kind because of its laudable purpose to produce "lower taxes down the line," as Feldstein asserts? It would be an interesting experiment to find out, but a costly one. In the meantime, the national debt would expand by nearly 50 percent, while the immediate financial condition of Social Security would not improve one jot.

Privatizers note that the costs of transitioning to a new system have been incurred in one form or another by numerous other countries, without lasting economic harm. The most frequently cited examples are Chile, Great Britain, and Sweden. All are said to have averted a near collapse of their traditional social insurance programs, and potentially of their economies, too, by supplanting them wholly or in part with private retirement systems. Unsurprisingly, the claims of unalloyed success for these transitions don't stand up to close scrutiny.

Of these three, Chile is the most heavily publicized example of a country that embarked on the right course. This is partially due to the tireless proselytizing of Jose Pinera, who was a government minister and created the system during the regime of Chilean dictator General Augusto Pinochet. From his perch at the Cato Institute, Pinera has been preaching the gospel of private retirement accounts for more than a decade. He has met with presidents and presidential contenders, among them Bill Clinton and then Texas governor George W. Bush. Energetically wholesaling his heartwarming tale of the little developing country that made good on its promise to retirees, he has single-handedly inflated his country's 1980 privatization experiment into a model admired all over the world.

Yet Chile's experience hardly provides a useful model for the United States. Chile's conventional pension system was on the verge of collapse in 1980—facing a genuine, not phony, financial crisis. The system was consuming ever-increasing subsidies from the government merely to stay afloat. Having evolved from a patchwork of separate systems for employees in different industries, it was an administrative morass that paid different benefits to workers in different walks of life. Even so, more than 90 percent of all workers received the bare minimum pension upon retirement.

Pinera scrapped the old system for all new workers save for one very privileged group: the military, which balked at the new mandate and backed up its objections by the exercise of brute political clout. Everyone else entering formal employment after 1981 was henceforth required to deposit 10 percent of earned wages in individual investment accounts managed by a handful of independent companies appointed by the Pinochet regime. Workers already enrolled in the old system were coerced and seduced into abandoning it by cuts in existing benefits and reductions in withholding taxes.

Chile financed the transition by tapping its sizable government surplus, an option plainly no longer available to the deficit-ridden U.S. government. During its first few years, an unprecedented bull market in Chilean stocks produced double-digit annual gains in portfolio values, seemingly validating the decision to subject workers' retirement funds to the vagaries of the market.

How much of these gains the workers will be able to pocket is questionable, however, for sky-high administrative fees have eaten deeply into worker accounts. Fully half the pension contributions of the average worker who retired in 2000 were consumed by fees, according to a survey by the World Bank. The bank calculated further that investment commissions charged by the independent management firms reduced workers' average annual rates of return between 1991 and 1995 from 12.9 percent to an unimpressive 2.1 percent. Although the government reformed the system in the mid-1990s to force commissions lower, in 2002 the fees still ranged from 12.2 percent to 25 percent of employee contributions. Because a large portion of the management costs were fixed, the higher percentages tended to be charged against the accounts of lower-wage workers.

The high fees were the consequence of the system's original design, as well as deficient government oversight. Chilean law narrowly constrains the investment choices that can be offered by the fund managers, which forces them to market essentially identical portfolios. Since no fund can compete with the others by promising superior investment returns, they poach customers from each other by offering expensive gifts for transferred accounts—toaster ovens, cell phones, television sets, even cash. These gifts, are, of course, fool's gold: their cost, and the expense of maintaining a marketing army that has been estimated to encompass as many as 20,000 salespersons, end up bundled into the fees and commissions that the workers pay. The fund managers, on the other hand, have done quite well by the system. In 1995, a year in which the investment return for new members dipped as low as negative 2.3 percent, the fund industry reported average profit margins of more than 21 percent. In some years, the industry profit margin has exceeded 50 percent.

Because the Chilean system covers only officially reported wages in a country with a large underground economy, half of the country's workers are still left without any pensions at all. Meanwhile, the first cohorts of retirees have been so disappointed with their benefits that political pressure is mounting on the government to provide subsidies. And many people resent that the military was the one class of workers that was permitted, thanks to General Pinochet's intercession, to continue to collect from the old defined-benefit system, which still pays well.

Sweden, once renowned for the generosity of its public pension system, also shifted to a partially privatized program in the late 1980s, in its case to respond to the pressure of changing demographics and a domestic economic crisis. About 10 percent of each worker's pension tax was henceforth placed in an investment account to be selected by the worker from among more than 650 mutual funds marketed by the country's aggressive financial firms. The change exposed the entire Swedish workforce to the domestic stock market, which swooned 68 percent from March 2000 through March 2003. By January 2004, some 84 percent of all private accounts were in the red.

Great Britain, which launched government-subsidized private pensions under the Thatcher government in 1988, has seen both risks and costs career out of control. In one of the biggest financial scandals in British history, some 2 million Britons have been cajoled into abandoning their secure government pensions in favor of private plans that provided them with lower benefits. The so-called mis-selling scandal resulted in the government's ordering insurance companies and other promoters of private accounts to refund more than $24 billion to their bilked clients. Meanwhile, the continuing doldrums of the British investment markets have provoked hundreds of thousands of customers to abandon their private plans and return to the government system—despite its reputation as one of the stingiest in Europe.

Despite the warnings implicit in these tales from abroad, not to mention the dubiousness of the basic economics of private accounts, the privateers continued through the 1990s to proclaim the superiority of private accounts over traditional Social Security. With the election of 2000, they finally gained an ally in the White House. As one of his very first acts in office, George W. Bush appointed a commission designed to grace the concept with an imprimatur of bipartisanism that proved to be, like so much else about the administration and privatization, wholly specious.

Chapter Eleven

Bush Stacks the Deck

Paul O'Neill was on the verge of relinquishing the chairmanship of Alcoa, the big aluminum company, and settling into a comfortable retirement with Nancy, his wife of 45 years, when George W. Bush's victory in the 2000 election changed his life.

On a Sunday in early December, one day after the U.S. Supreme Court announced its intention to step into the election controversy raging over the voting results in Florida, he received a call from his old friend Dick Cheney, inviting him to Washington to meet the Republican president-in-waiting. Barely two weeks later, he had agreed to become secretary of the Treasury in the new Republican administration.

O'Neill would reveal later that he had accepted the job largely to pursue one of the great ambitions of his late career, the reform of Social Security. He had been encouraged in this endeavor by his old friend Alan Greenspan, who shared his concern that the approaching wave of baby-boomer retirements would drive the program into bankruptcy. The only option, O'Neill thought, was to junk the New Deal program and replace it with something entirely modern—something like a program designed around individual retirement accounts.

So when he received the call from Dick Cheney he was hard-pressed to rebuff the overture. He knew that the president-elect favored privatizing Social Security, at least in principle—he had made it an important plank in the recent campaign, energetically with Al Gore, his Democratic opponent, over tangling Social Security's condition. If George Bush was already thinking about private accounts, O'Neill was ready with a proposal.

He floated it during his very first meeting with the president-elect in a Washington office. O'Neill's version of Social Security privatization was the creation of what he called "wealth accumulation accounts"—nest eggs that would be granted instead of Social Security to every worker under the age of 35 or so, under conditions that would allow the funds to appreciate to $1 million by retirement. To his bemusement, Bush brushed him off, as though he couldn't be bothered to waste time on the details since he had already expressed his commitment to privatization. O'Neill tried not to let Bush's incuriousness faze him. The new president was open to radical reform of Social Security, that was clear enough. He recalled leaving the meeting "convinced . . . that it was appropriate for me to accept the challenge to return to public service."

But Bush had not even taken the oath of office before O'Neill grew concerned that his fiscal philosophy might be out of sync with the incoming administration. He was especially uneasy about the White House's insistence on placing a huge tax cut at the head of its domestic agenda. He feared that the draining of trillions of dollars from the Treasury would cripple his Social Security fix, which would require massive funding in the short term. The budget surplus that Bill Clinton had bequeathed the Bush administration was estimated to be $5 trillion over ten years, but the proposed tax cut would suck up almost a third of that. If the economy soured at all (and the leading indicators were beginning to forecast heavy weather), there would be scant money left for his rescue mission. As O'Neill recalled thinking at the time, the surplus represented a "historic, maybe once-in-a-lifetime" chance to save the system. "It was now or never." And the chance was already slipping away.

As things worked out, O'Neill would never have much opportunity to hold the president's ear on economic matters in general or Social Security in particular. He and Bush never seemed to connect on a personal level. O'Neill certainly never got used to the way that an idea, once locked into Bush's mind, couldn't be jarred loose.

At one Oval Office meeting in March 2001, O'Neill finally got the chance to lay out his plan for private accounts, after he had worked out the details with Greenspan. The existing Social Security system would be maintained for all workers over 37. Younger workers would have the option to invest their payroll tax in a mix of stock and bond index funds. He and Greenspan had concluded that the transition could be undertaken for $1 trillion. Bush seemed to be thrown by the particulars, although it wasn't clear whether that was because the age cutoff was too low or because the whole system didn't sufficiently resemble the conventional private retirement accounts that had been plugged by conservatives since the 1980s. For whatever reason, Bush cut O'Neill short. "I didn't go with that approach in the campaign," he said, and then seemed to stop listening.

O'Neill emerged from the meeting frustrated and demoralized. "I'm the Treasury Secretary and I happen to have spent forty years studying Social Security," he vented later. "The Fed chairman and I are in agreement. . . . But [Bush] just sat back in his chair. His attitude was, 'I said this during the campaign, and whatever I said in the campaign must be right.' "

It was just one more in a series of unsettling encounters. O'Neill had become profoundly alienated by the bare-knuckled political calculation of the White House team. Nothing exemplified this as much as the way they went about crafting what they called the President's Commission to Strengthen Social Security.

Much would be riding on this blue-ribbon committee. For all Bush believed that his campaign push for private retirement accounts had helped him get elected, there were widespread doubts among policy makers and the public about replacing even a small portion of Social Security with individual accounts. Convening a respected, bipartisan council to air the pros and cons in public would do wonders to establish privatization as a responsible approach to Social Security reform. O'Neill was absolutely confident that the reform made such obvious economic sense that reasoned public discourse would quell all public doubt.

White House political operators like Karl Rove, however, viewed all policy through the prism of ideology. To them, public debate was a tedious formality, best dispensed with altogether. O'Neill thought this attitude was particularly dangerous when the subject was Social Security, on which there was as yet no popular consensus—or to be precise, on which popular consensus was split along generational and partisan lines.

In creating the Commission to Strengthen Social Security, the White House appeared to be totally ignorant of the lessons to be drawn from Alan Greenspan's 1983 commission, which had been genuinely bipartisan and empowered to propose policy changes of any kind—and which had been perhaps the most accomplished reform panel in Social Security's history. Instead of sharing appointing authority with Republicans and Democrats in Congress, as Reagan had done in establishing the 1983 panel, Bush filled all 16 seats himself (although they were divided between nominal Republicans and Democrats). As its very title implied, this wasn't to be just *any* Social Security commission; it was the *president's* commission.

O'Neill was dismayed by the manner in which the White House chose the commissioners. To make sure that they all supported privatization, every candidate was carefully screened by Rove or Larry Lindsey, a top White House economic adviser whom O'Neill privately considered to be an intellectual lightweight. "It meant we gave away our most valuable asset, credibility," O'Neill said later. "If you're certain you're right—and I think we are on private accounts—you shouldn't be afraid to include the opposing voices at your table. . . . In this case, we should have been confident enough to engage the other side."

There were other signs of the White House's determination to stack the commission. Seven of the original appointees came from the corporate or financial services world, two from the Cato Institute—but not one from organized labor. Two members had served on the 1994 advisory council, where they had supported Sylvester Schieber's private account scheme: Carolyn Weaver of the conservative American Enterprise Institute, and Fidel Vargas, who was no longer a boy mayor from southern California but an executive in an investment firm. (Weaver never actually took office; her place was taken two months into the commission's deliberations by Leanne Abdnor, a former Cato vice president who had set up the Alliance for Worker Retirement Security as a front for the National Association of Manufacturers. Her appointment gave Cato nearly one-fifth of the commission seats.)

The co-chairmen were Richard D. Parsons, then the chief operating officer of AOL Time Warner (he would later become its chairman and CEO), and Senator Daniel Moynihan, a staunch defender of Social Security whose presence lent the commission the misleading glow of bipartisanship, but who would soon chafe under the White House's heavy-handed control of the agenda.

O'Neill was certainly correct about the commission's credibility. It had none. The day its membership was announced, the Senate Democratic leader, Tom Daschle, labeled it a "stacked, completely orchestrated effort to come to a desired result. . . . There has been no effort to achieve balance, no effort to reach out and try to ensure that it is an objective review."

An even better indication of the commission's lack of stature was that, other than Daschle's broadside, the announcement of the appointees generated almost no Washington buzz. The panel looked to be just another phony Bush stage set. Indeed, the commission's makeup would ensure that any proposals it made would be dead on arrival in a divided Congress.

The commissioners themselves evidently perceived their equivocal position from the beginning. In convening the first official meeting on June 11, Parsons complained about the public's skepticism of their independence. "There are a number of people who have already begun to attack the work of this commission even though this is our first meeting," he said. "They're out rattling their sabers and threatening—or charging us with committing all sorts of mayhem upon retired Americans or disabled

Americans or future generations of Americans, when we haven't proposed any approach to the problem yet."

But he was being disingenuous. The "approach to the problem" had been explicitly dictated by the Bush administration in the commission's formal charter. Their hands were more than merely tied; they were manacled to a set of six presidential "principles" that, among other things, ruled out a payroll tax increase, barred investments by the Social Security trust fund in the stock market, and mandated that any solution include private accounts.

Privatization advocates insisted that the commission was free to do its work with an open mind. As Andrew Biggs of the Cato Institute, a commission staff member, later wrote, the ground rules "did not dictate the commission's conclusions." They were "flexible enough" to be "anything but preordained."

The truth is that the commission's "flexibility" was a charade. Its members were predisposed toward cutting benefits and replacing them, as far as might be possible, with the proceeds of private accounts. They seemed nearly unanimous in the conviction that every owner of an individual retirement account would be equally capable of capturing the same lavish stock market returns that had been recorded in recent years, and that these would improve every retiree's lot over what the traditional system offered—although one commissioner, Professor Olivia S. Mitchell of the Wharton School of Business, had published a study indicating that many households would do no better under privatization than under the existing system.

One can scour the transcripts of the panel's seven public sessions in vain for a word of dissent, or even a hint that any member felt that the federal social insurance program that had functioned so successfully for more than six decades had earned the right to be presumed worth saving.

Nor did the Social Security Administration itself have a seat at the table. This was a major departure from past practice. Through the years, the support staffs of advisory councils and presidential commissions had almost always been drawn from the Social Security bureaucracy and supervised by a program official. One could object that this tradition had allowed the bureaucrats to manipulate several generations of appointed commissioners, but on the plus side it ensured that the program's history, tradition, and institutional memory could not be cavalierly dismissed.

In this case, the staff was supervised by a director hostile to the program's basic principles: Charles P. Blahous, a former Senate Republican staff aide whose previous post had been executive director of the Alliance for Worker Retirement Security, Leanne Abdnor's pro-privatization NAM front group.

The members relied for their basic information on voluminous packets of studies and analyses prepared by Blahous and his staff, but it would be unfair to say that he led them by the nose. On the contrary, the transcripts show that the commissioners were enthusiastic consumers of the staff's one-sided presentations, almost never challenging their core assumptions. Uncontradicted, the tenets of privatization were reinforced in the commission's echo chamber until they acquired the halo of received truth. These included the assumption that the program would start running a cash deficit in 2016 and become insolvent in 2038, based on the intermediate projection of the 2001 trustees' report.* No one took pains during the commission's

---

*These dates moved further back in time with subsequent trustees' reports. The intermediate projection of the 2004 report placed them at 2018 and 2042, respectively.

plenary sessions to explain the uncertainties underlying the intermediate forecasts, or to point out that the trustees had issued alternative projections, including one that painted a relatively optimistic picture of the future.

The question of how changes in economic conditions might affect Social Security's fiscal balance rarely came up in discussion. When it did, the issue was likely to be waved away, as when Commissioner Robert Pozen, an executive at Fidelity Investments, admonished his colleagues that "it's not possible to grow out of this problem"—an assertion contradicted by the trustees' best-case scenario, which showed that achievable gains in productivity, inflation, and other variables could produce permanent solvency for the system without any legislated changes in taxes or benefits.

Steve Goss, the Social Security Administration's chief actuary, did attend almost every session. He remained a largely silent presence in public, although he impressed the panel with his habit of answering their technical queries with emails dispatched in the dead of night. ("When does he sleep?" Mitchell asked at one point.)

Very occasionally, and very tactfully, Goss would inject himself into the commission's deliberations to correct a flagrant misconception. When Commissioner Robert Johnson, the founder and chairman of Black Entertainment Television and an inexperienced navigator of the Social Security thicket, repeated the cherished canard that African-American workers are cheated by the system because "they die off faster" than whites, Goss gingerly set him straight.

"If you look solely just at the retirement benefits, you are absolutely right," he said. But he informed Johnson that African-American men have higher disability rates than whites and that

that factor, along with black families' higher reliance on dependent and survivor benefits, tended to compensate for their mortality losses from the old-age program. He might have continued in the same vein, but Blahous interrupted with a request to "wrap this up."

It remains unclear how much of the commission's output was the product of its own deliberations and how much was provided in premasticated form by Blahous and his staff. By the time of the panel's first meeting on June 11, convened minutes after the commissioners' swearing-in ceremony, the staff already had been working in high gear on the commission's official "interim" report. In accordance with the president's instructions, a draft of the report was to be published within a few weeks, even before the commission would have a chance to meet a second time. The interim report's purpose was to educate the public about "the magnitude, the timing, and the scope of the problem . . . and what the consequences of failing to act are," as one commissioner remarked. The notion that the magnitude, timing, and scope of the problem might be debatable never came up in, well, debate.

The commission's two-hour conference with Blahous that afternoon formed the extent of its participation as a body in drafting the interim report. If any members wished to apply some critical analysis to the staff's precooked conclusions—the situation was dire, private accounts the answer—they failed to speak up.

When the draft appeared in July, it resembled a manifesto drawn from orthodox privatization doctrine, predictably brimming with outrageous misrepresentations. These included the usual assertions that the trust fund was valueless; that the program's vaunted progressivity, which favored low-wage workers over the better-paid, was largely imaginary; and that (Goss's ex-

planation notwithstanding) the program systematically defrauded African Americans of their just deserts.

The document compared the coming funding crisis, which
was at least 47 years off by the trustees' own estimate, with the
1983 crisis, in which the system had come within weeks of genuine insolvency. It offered charts full of optimistic projections of
the appreciation of even a modest private account—forecasting,
for instance, that an annual contribution of only $500 would
grow, over 40 years and compounded at a 4 percent real interest
rate, into $50,000. It didn't add that four decades of inflation
might reduce that nest egg to the present-day equivalent of about
$8,000, or mention that Social Security's benefits, in contrast,
are inflation-proof, or project the investment gains using risk-adjusted returns.

Almost as soon as the draft was published, Parsons and
Moynihan were placed on the defensive. Within 24 hours, a
team of four economists convened by the liberal Century Foundation had picked the document apart point-by-point. The two
sides traded barbs for a couple of days before the discussion pe-
tered out. But when the final version of the interim report was
issued a few weeks later, many of the most extreme misstatements had been removed.

Nothing disturbed the commission's complacent acceptance
of private accounts as the be-all and end-all of Social Security
reform until October 18, five months into their deliberations,
when Alicia Munnell, a retirement expert from Boston College
and one of the Century Foundation critics, tried to jar them off
their predetermined path. Invited to address the commission as
part of a panel of economists, Munnell opened her formal statement by reminding the members that Social Security had been

designed to insulate retirees from the vicissitudes of the economic cycle, not to increase their exposure.

"Individual accounts will not solve Social Security's long-run financial problem, and they are unduly risky for people's basic retirement benefit," she told them. She evoked the traditional three-pillar analogy that represented the stable guaranteed benefits of Social Security as one element of a secure retirement program to be complemented by private pension plans and personal savings. Substituting another set of personal savings for the secure defined benefit, Munnell said, would eliminate the protection from risk that was the program's true raison d'être. She reminded the panel that Social Security provides the majority of income for two-thirds of its recipients and was the sole source of sustenance for a third: "Retirement income that depends on one's skills as an investor is not consistent with the basic goals of a mandatory social security program," she concluded.

If Munnell's words shook any of the members loose from their preconceptions, they didn't show it. When the commission's final report appeared two months later, it was apparent that her words had not made the slightest impression.

Throughout its deliberations, the 2001 commission publicly exhibited a remarkable level of collegiality and mutual respect. But this concealed a small drama behind the scenes involving Moynihan, who had apparently begun to wonder whether he had unwittingly lent his name and reputation to an ideological swindle.

It is unclear whether Moynihan, who died in 2003, had been led to believe that he would have a free hand in setting the commission's course, or whether he misunderstood how strictly his co-chairman Parsons and the other commissioners would hew to the rules imposed by the Bush administration. Either way, by late in the fall he had become restive about the influence that Blahous and the White House exercised over the deliberations.

Moynihan communicated his feelings to staff members at the Treasury Department, who promptly passed the information to O'Neill by memo. "Moynihan has expressed a considerable amount of frustration that he is not being allowed to control the agenda," one wrote to the Treasury secretary on October 15, "and, in particular, that the White House and Commission Staff are controlling the agenda to a large extent."

A week later, he amplified his thoughts, expressing concern that some valued Democratic constituencies, including labor unions and the American Association of Retired Persons, had questioned his participation in what looked like an effort to "dismantle Social Security." Moynihan became particularly irked at an attempt by the administration to add an entirely new reform proposal to the agenda in November, a month before the commission's final report was due. This was a plan to deposit $10,000 in cash into a personal account for any 21-year-old willing to forego three-quarters of his or her future Social Security benefits. (The proposal never made it into the final report.)

Moynihan feared that the commission's advocacy of private accounts might be construed as "radical" reform, rather than as a natural outgrowth of the reforms he had been advocating since the Clinton administration. His resentment of what he saw as the White House's hijacking of the commission agenda seems almost touching in its naiveté: in fact, the White House had controlled the agenda from the get-go.

It's not clear whether Moynihan ever expressed his concerns to his fellow commissioners. "I never sensed any such attitude from the senator," Mitchell stated later. "Rather, he was always energetic, funny, supportive, cooperative, creative, engaged, and a true leader."

In public, he presented a united front with his colleagues to the end. On December 11, he joined them in a unanimous public vote adopting the final report, which laid out three alternative models for private retirement accounts that required as much as $3 trillion in government budget transfers. As O'Neill had feared, the report was received in Washington with a vast, open-mouthed yawn, although not entirely for the reasons he foresaw.

It was true that the preordained character of the proposals had drained them of drama. But official Washington also understood that the administration's spending binge following the September 11 attacks made the prospects slim for any large-scale funding for Social Security reform. Politicians of both parties, meanwhile, quailed at the very idea of dealing with as explosive an issue as Social Security so close to the 2002 midterm elections. The reform wouldn't occupy the front burner of domestic politics for at least another year.

For all these reasons, the next day's newspapers buried the story—the *New York Times* on page 27, the *Washington Post* on page 33, the *Wall Street Journal* on page 20. Most coverage interpreted the three-option package as a retreat from President Bush's original mandate that the commission produce one plan to be railroaded through Congress on a single vote. Several stories quoted Moynihan asserting defensively that he and Parsons had received permission from the president personally, during a meeting in the Oval Office, to present multiple options.

Any one of the three proposals, if enacted, would work the most radical change on Social Security in the program's history.

The commission's so-called Model 1, the least ambitious,

would allow a worker to voluntarily divert up to 2 percentage points of his or her payroll tax (that is, slightly less than one-third of the employee share of 6.2 percent) into a private investment account. It would reduce the worker's future Social Security benefits by the amount of the shift compounded at a rate of 3.5 percent a year above inflation. In other words, workers with private accounts would be better off than those who remained in the original program as long as their accounts appreciated at that rate. Model 1 involved no other benefit cuts or tax increases and therefore would do nothing to improve Social Security's financial health. Because of the diversion of tax revenues to private accounts, the commission acknowledged, Model 1 would hasten the program's insolvency, leaving it out of money by the 2030s.

Model 2 would allow workers to divert 4 percent of their pay, up to a maximum of $1,000 a year, into a private account. (The ceiling would be adjusted upward every year.) The contributions would also be offset by benefit reductions, but at a lower rate, 2 percent compounded annually, than in Model 1. Model 2 also cut conventional benefits drastically for all recipients by changing the formula used to calculate Social Security's initial retirement stipend.

Model 3 was the most elaborate option. It allowed workers to shift 2.5 percent of their pay from the payroll tax into private accounts, as long as they added another 1 percent to the accounts out of their own pockets. The voluntary add-on would be subsidized by the government through a progressive tax credit that provided relatively greater benefits to lower-paid workers. This plan also reduced the basic retirement benefit overall, although not as sharply as Model 2, by tinkering with various program formulas. The commission calculated that workers with private accounts would do better than the holdouts if their accounts earned 2.5 percent a year over inflation.

The commission certified that all three plans met President Bush's specifications—they were designed around private accounts, avoided a payroll tax increase, and permitted no government investment in the stock market. Of the three, however, the commission plainly favored Model 2.

Model 1 set an unrealistically high bar for profitability of the private accounts. A 3.5 percent return after inflation meant that a worker's portfolio would have to consistently earn 6.5 or 7 percent a year, a difficult objective for a diversified portfolio of stocks and bonds. The plan did nothing to achieve long-term financial stability for the system. Most economists who analyzed the commission proposals in the following months all but ignored it.

Model 3 was overly complicated. The mandated additional out-of-pocket worker contribution would be a serious obstacle for workers who already were hard-pressed to save for their retirements. The proposal also required continuing cash infusions from the federal budget, clearly a major drawback.

Model 2 received the greatest public scrutiny. Its benchmark of a 2 percent return after inflation was arguably an attainable goal, even for investors who shunned the stock market; government securities routinely yield 3 percent above inflation.

But it wasn't long before critics focused on the one provision of Model 2 that produced a truly dramatic and troubling change in the Social Security program. This was a deceptively simple shift from the "wage indexing" to "price indexing" of initial retirement benefits. Deceptively simple, because it was this provision, not the private accounts, that produced almost all of the plan's fiscal savings for the Social Security system.

As Social Security works today, a new retiree's initial monthly benefit is derived from a formula based on his or her highest-earning 35 years of work, automatically adjusted for wage growth over that period. The idea is to hold the so-called replacement rate—the percentage of a worker's final wages represented by the initial benefit—at a reasonably steady level as new retirees enter the system each year.

Reflecting the system's progressive character, the replacement rate is higher for lower-earning than higher-earning workers. For workers retiring in 2005, it was about 73 percent for the lowest one-fifth of wage earners, 43 percent for average earners, and 28.5 percent for the highest-paid fifth. (That is, a worker earning an average of $10,000 a year toward the end of his or her career would receive initial Social Security benefits of about $7,300 a year, and so on.)

After the initial benefit is set, monthly payments are indexed for inflation so that a retiree's purchasing power won't erode over time.

Because wage growth has almost always exceeded inflation, wage-indexing means that initial Social Security benefits tend to improve in lock-step with economic growth—in other words, retirees "share in the general increase in the standard of living that society as a whole experiences from one generation to the next," as the economists Peter Diamond and Peter R. Orszag have observed. Wage indexing cushions the jolt downward in lifestyle that often comes with the shift from living on wages to life on a pension, especially for lower-paid workers.

Changing to a system of price indexing would shatter this trend. Increases in initial retirement benefits would track inflation, not economic growth. The change would freeze the standard of living of Social Security retirees at whatever level prevailed the year the policy went into effect. As economist

Edward Gramlich, the chairman of the 1994 advisory council, noted, if price indexing had been in place when the first Social Security recipients got their first checks, retirees "would be living today at 1940 living standards." The number of elderly living in poverty would be triple the number today—more than 10 million, or 30 percent of people aged 65 and over.

Not only would anyone retiring on a Social Security pension suffer a drop in living standards the moment he or she stopped working, but the gap would widen over time. A Congressional Budget Office study showed that even for average earners with private accounts, the replacement rate under Model 2 would drop by half over 60 years, from 43 percent for the 2005 class of retirees (almost exactly where it was in 1939) to 21.7 percent in the retirement year 2065. Thirty years after that, the replacement rate for average earners would be just over 10 percent.

For low-wage retirees, the replacement rate would decline to the point where a Social Security benefit would be scarcely large enough to keep a worker out of poverty. Eventually, Social Security would replace such a meager portion of a person's working wages that the program would simply wither away.

The commission defended the change by noting that automatic wage indexing wasn't part of the original Social Security system, but was added by Congress in 1977. This is true, but misleading.

Before automatic indexing, Congress revised benefits every couple of years to adjust them to recent economic trends, invariably raising them to reflect rising wage rates and protect beneficiaries from inflation. The 1977 reform may have placed this burdensome political chore on autopilot, but it was designed to match what Congress had always done manually in the past.

If price indexing would save Social Security all by itself, why then did the commission need to propose individual accounts—especially given that they would add as much as $4.7 trillion in transition costs to the Social Security system, as some analysts calculated? The commission's rationale was that the investment gains earned by account holders were to compensate for the benefit cuts—in fact, they were the only mechanism that could make up for the cuts.

The flaw in that argument is that the commission made no effort to recognize the investment risk faced by account holders, many of whom were sure to have absolutely no experience in the securities markets. As Diamond and Orszag observed, not "a single mention of the increased risk associated with a diversified portfolio" appears in the entire 256-page report. For all the commission cared, the workers would be on their own.

Chapter Twelve

Operation Shock and Awe

T HE FIRST resounding cannonade of George W. Bush's second-term campaign against Social Security was fired by a balding, baby-faced aide to Karl Rove named Peter Wehner. The 44-year-old Wehner was the kind of White House assistant whose name is almost never heard in public unless an enterprising Washington reporter gins up a soft profile to ensure that his phone calls will henceforth get returned. By custom and convention the profile will depict the subject as "quiet and soft-spoken"; a devoted family man ("home for dinner by 6:30 p.m."); unassertive yet intellectually persuasive in the councils of government ("he doesn't overstate, and his arguments have a lot of integrity"); and a believer not in the bludgeon and mace of partisan politics, but in the "power of ideas."

The *Washington Post* profile of Wehner published shortly after the 2004 election, from which these phrases are taken, followed form in depicting him as a sort of Republican Adlai Stevenson. But Wehner was a Rove man through and through, an acolyte to someone whose name has become synonymous with ruthless partisanship. At the beginning of 2005, Social Security was in his crosshairs. On January 3, as the New Year's Eve bunting was coming down around the nation's capital and the inauguration scaffolding was going up on the Capitol mall, he drafted a bellicose memorandum to inform the administration's right-wing power base precisely where the privatizing of Social Security fit in the White House's worldview.

"The debate about Social Security is going to be a monumental clash of ideas—and it's important for the conservative movement that we win both the battle of ideas and the legislation that will give those ideas life," Wehner wrote. "At the end of the day, we want to promote both an ownership society and advance the idea of limited government." The dismantling of Social Security would be the final unmaking of the New Deal: "For the first time in six decades, the Social Security battle is one we can win—and in doing so, we can help transform the political and philosophical landscape of the country. Increasingly the Democrat [sic] Party is the party of obstruction and opposition. It is the Party of the Past."

The GOP would emerge from the fray as the party of the future. "Greater opportunity, more freedom, and more control for individuals over their own lives," Wehner wrote. "That is what the personal account debate is fundamentally about—and it is clearly the crucial new conservative idea in the history of the Social Security debate."

Wehner threw in a few economic tidbits to sustain the pretense that fiscal issues lay at the heart of the debate, but they were boilerplate lies. The system is on an "unsustainable course." It confronts "more than $10 trillion in unfunded liabilities." It is "heading for an iceberg."

If there were any remaining doubts that Bush's campaign against Social Security was not fiscal or economic but strictly ideological, Wehner's memo dispelled them in a stroke. But his words weren't meant for the public eye (although they were promptly leaked to the press). In its public language, the Bush campaign for Social Security reform was not so candid. It stuck to addressing the program's financial condition by repeating the point that the magic of privatization would save the program from bankruptcy; never was heard a single word about the goal of ensuring victory for the conservative movement in "the battle of ideas."

In launching what amounted to a new domestic version of Operation Shock and Awe, the White House spared no ordnance. As the persuader-in-chief, the president himself undertook to criss-cross the country, reiterating at dozens of stage-managed events his sanctimonious regret at the obsolescence of the once grand and effective program and his determination to give it a twenty-first-century polish.

Karl Rove's astroturf front group, Progress for America, flexed muscles that were pumped up with wads of corporate donations. The organization signed up Thomas Saving, a pro-privatization ringer serving on the Social Security Board of Trustees, as a consultant and spokesman. "I already do an awful lot of speeches about Social Security and Medicare," Saving, an economics professor at Texas A&M University, cheerily informed the *Houston Chronicle*. Perhaps wary of being thought stodgy, the organization also drafted one Noah McCullough, a 9-year-old master of memorized presidential trivia, as a sort of curtain-raising act for the president's road show. ("What I want to tell people about Social Security is to not be afraid of the new plan," said young McCullough. "It may be a change, but it's a good change.")

The White House was not above deploying Social Security's own credibility as a weapon against its own interests. The Social Security Administration's letters to contributors and retirees, its annual trustee reports, even the recorded messages played for callers on hold were rewritten to bemoan the program's impending doom and plump for the administration's peculiar version of reform. Agency employees presently complained to Congress that they had been directed to "spread a political message intended to 'scare the public about the future of Social Security,'" prompting a query from congressional Democrats to Social Security commissioner Jo Anne Barnhart, a Bush appointee. Barnhart assured them that "the messages we use to inform the public have been consistent throughout the past decade."

The minority staff promptly compared the public materials the system disseminated in 2005 to those issued in 2001 or earlier (that is, under previous administrations), and determined Barnhart's words to be flatly untrue. To the contrary, they found a "growing politicization" of even the most routine communications. Although the program's fiscal condition had actually improved during the first Bush term, the tone and language of its communications had grown steadily more grim, until nothing was left but unrelieved warnings of "a massive and growing shortfall" that rendered the system "unsustainable."

The 2000 version of the system's most basic public primer had begun with the question, "Will Social Security be there for you?" and the answer, "Absolutely." By 2005 the Q&A had been dropped, supplanted by the admonition that "Social Security must change to meet future challenges." Even the annual statements mailed to taxpayers had turned ominous. The 2001 statement had reminded recipients of Social Security's "major role" in keeping the elderly out of poverty. By 2005, this and other similar reassurances were gone, replaced with dire warnings of the system's impending collapse "unless action is taken soon."

As the president sallied forth on his grand speaking tour, the privatization faithful were convening at what one might consider the libertarian St. Peter's Basilica, the six-story postmodern Cato Institute headquarters on Massachusetts Avenue in Washington, D.C.

On Social Security privatization, Cato is the center of the universe. For 25 years the rightist think tank has been a relentless promoter of private accounts and the fount of hundreds of white papers, book-length studies, and op-eds driving the battle plan. The institute had kept the spark alive against long odds for so many years that its leadership still seemed a little uneasy about ceding the issue to the White House, as though it is still waiting for Bush & Co. to prove their ideological bona fides before fully letting go.

Accordingly, in Washington during the second week of February 2005, the institute convened its own two-day conference on Social Security reform, Cato-style. "This conference isn't about 'Should you privatize,'" Michael Tanner, the chairman of its Social Security task force, told me when, perhaps naively, I asked him why there wasn't a single privatization skeptic, much less an opponent (or a Democrat), listed among the more than two dozen speakers. "We wanted a discussion within the family about *how* to do it, not to get into another debate about *whether* we should do it."

Tanner is an earnest man with a receding hairline, a silver-and-black goatee, and a jeweled stud glinting incongruously from his left earlobe. If there's a benign face of privatization, it's his. Tanner is most at his ease making philosophical arguments, not engaging in ad hominem fisticuffs. One rarely finds him predicting the extermination of the Democratic Party, sliming the AARP, or engaging in any of the other White House dirty tricks that threaten to turn Social Security reform into another of Karl Rove's scorched-earth crusades. Not long after the conference, when Tanner was forced to share a studio appearance on CNN with USA Next's thuggish chairman Charles Jarvis, his body language suggested that his sheer proximity to Jarvis was making his skin crawl. When he was asked about a USA Next Internet ad that accused AARP of supporting gay marriage, he called it disappointing and "bigoted."

Tanner's role as Cato's Social Security spearhead dates to 1995, when he took over its task force on the topic. Cato had established its episcopate over privatization years earlier, publishing its first book-length tract, *Social Security: The Inherent Contradiction* by a Harvard law student named Peter Ferraro, in 1980, and following up with the "Leninist" manifesto about undermining public support for Social Security in 1983.

For much of that period the political environment hadn't seemed ripe for dramatic reform. Then the weather began to change.

"What brought it back was the 1994 advisory council under Clinton," Tanner recalled. This was the council at which Robert Ball made his last stand against privatization. Conservatives had found encouragement in the fact that, even if the panel hadn't managed to produce a legislative proposal, a majority of its members had endorsed one or the other of the two private-account solutions it had reviewed.

For the next few years, privatization advocates rode a political roller-coaster. Some, including Tanner, are convinced that Bill Clinton was on the verge of proposing a carve-out plan in 1998 when the Lewinsky scandal knocked if off track.

"Why would that have had anything to do with it?" I asked him.

"He had to move to the left," he replied. In fact, there's no evidence that Clinton was preparing to propose anything like a diversion of payroll tax revenues to private accounts. The most Clinton is known to have considered was an add-on option granting tax deductions and possibly a federal subsidy for voluntary accounts designed to complement, not replace, Social Security.

The year 2001 brought more disappointment to the privatization faithful. Stacked with privatization advocates, President Bush's reform commission had been rigged to provide private accounts with a veneer of bipartisan respectability. The panel's final report that fall was to be a legislative blueprint for the following congressional session. Then came 9/11. The report appeared two months later, greeted in Washington by almost total silence. Domestic policy was stricken from the president's agenda for the next three years.

As though impelled by its own momentum, Cato continued to press the issue. In 2001 it sponsored three conferences and forums on Social Security. In 2002, a year in which the issue was overwhelmed by the waging of one overseas war and preparations for another, Cato bravely soldiered on with 11 events. From Tanner's descriptions I was led to imagine desultory gatherings attended by a few true believers and sideshow seekers. The experience seemed to have marked him; he sounded like a general who, having had victory slip out of his grasp many times before, finally senses the prize within reach—but still fears that something might yet go wrong.

For the record, he assured me that he thought things were looking up. The White House had signaled that Bush wasn't going to back off from Social Security reform this time—he was going to stump for privatization every week for two months straight, until the nation was behind him. Rove-affiliated front groups such as USA Next had announced plans to drum up as much as $100 million in cash for television advertising. "I'm stunned at the level at which they're treating this," Tanner said of the White House. "They're pulling out all the stops. It's going to be virtually like a presidential campaign." Cato, naturally, would be in the thick of it. "We see our role as providing intellectual ammunition for the debate," he said.

He also left no room for doubt that Cato, like Peter Wehner, saw the issue in terms of ideology, not economics—as a classic battle to promote libertarian ideals, which were hostile to the very notion of social insurance. "In the end, this isn't a debate about the system's solvency in 2018 or 2042," he said dismissively. "It's about whether you think the government should be in control of your retirement or people should take ownership and responsibility. That's why the debate is so intense—why would anyone get so excited about transition costs? This is about whether we redefine a relationship between individuals and government that we've had since 1935. We say that what was done was wrong then, and it's wrong now. Our position is that people need to be responsible for their own lives."

The next morning, a chilly Tuesday, Edward H. Crane, Cato's burly and florid founder and chairman, stepped to the podium in the institute's Frederick A. Hayek Auditorium (named for a hero of laissez-faire economics) to open the conference. The audience filled the 300-seat hall and overflowed into the foyer outside, where a bank of chairs was set up in front of a closed-circuit TV screen.

The conference program all but glowed with the light of a galaxy of privatization stars. The first day's keynote address was delivered by Martin Feldstein, the academic patriarch of privatization. Names familiar to anyone who had spent time hacking through the thickets of debate dotted the speaker's list: Leanne Abdnor, founder of the Alliance for Worker Retirement Security, the manufacturing lobby's astroturf front; Derrick Max, the alliance's executive director and the newly-designated chief of an industry fundraising campaign launched by Rove and his associates; Social Security Commissioner Saving, not yet appointed to his speech-making gig by Progress for America; and the ubiquitous Andrew Biggs, late of Cato and the 2001 commission, now ensconced inside Social Security headquarters as an associate commissioner.

Five GOP lawmakers were to deliver a tag-team assessment of the prospects for legislation on Capitol Hill. (Tanner expressed disappointment that for some reason he hadn't been able to persuade a Democrat to join the fun.) A sixth Republican, Senator Rick Santorum of Pennsylvania, was scheduled to deliver the second-day luncheon address, the obligatory tub-thumping attack on the Democratic Party, which he would describe as so wrong-headed in its determination to confound the public's wishes that it risked being hounded into extinction by an outraged electorate.

Crane's role was to give a succinct Dick-and-Jane preview of the next two days. He touched on several motifs that would recur often in the hours to come, a couple of which were new to me. A major talking point was something called *Flemming v. Nestor*, which turned out to be a U.S. Supreme Court case that excites a conditioned response in every red-blooded privateer. The Court ruled in this 1960 decision that payroll tax contributions, unlike insurance policy premiums, don't give taxpayers a legal claim to any specific Social Security benefits upon retirement.

One would have thought this was self-evident, for the same reason that paying income tax doesn't entitle a taxpayer to any specific level or kind of service, either. But to the privateers, *Flemming v. Nestor* is as close to a bill of indictment as Social Security has ever come. As Crane put it, the Court ruled that "what you get back [from your payroll tax] is entirely up to the whim of 535 politicians" in the Senate and House of Representatives.

Crane didn't follow his own train of thought to ask what the chances might be that 535 politicians dependent on voters for their jobs would arbitrarily throttle Social Security, or how that probability would measure up to the likelihood that the stock market's value might arbitrarily ratchet down by 10 percent or 20 percent, as it had done in three of the previous five years. It was enough to know that Congress had the legal right to skin the working person; to a libertarian conditioned to mistrust politicians even in the best circumstances, *Flemming v. Nestor* looked like a ticking time bomb. Over the next two days it seemed that scarcely a single panel failed to mention the case at least once.

Crane next touched on the trust fund and its worthless IOUs, intoning by rote the privatization lobby's mantra: "The trust fund is broke. The reality is there are no assets in any trust fund. A lot of pieces of paper," only government bonds, etc.

This viewpoint, however, did cast a strange light on his next point, which was that Cato's favored reform would award something called "recognition bonds" to workers who had already paid Social Security taxes but wanted to throw in their lot with private accounts. The recognition bonds, which would be inheritable assets, would represent the value of their prior payroll contributions and would be issued as a substitute for benefit claims. As Crane described them, however, they sounded awfully like Treasury bonds—IOUs very similar to the securities owned by the trust fund. Why they would have value while the trust fund's assets did not was something I waited to hear Crane explain, but in vain. Nobody raised this point from the audience, either.

This provided my first glimpse of the downside of the echo chamber approach to policy making. Inconsistencies and contradictions that would get wrung out through honest and vigorous debate get worked so deeply into the fabric of the ideology that they become invisible, except to an outsider.

There would be many more examples of the echo chamber at work over the next two days. Leanne Abdnor would open her panel by describing how thoroughly dependent on Social Security widows and divorced women were, then offer a prescription to sharply cut guaranteed benefits and replace them with a flyer in the stock market. William Shipman, a dapper former investment banker who is the high priest of the movement's stock-market-as-savior church, proposed a private account system based on the diversion of 2 percentage points of the payroll tax that he called "basically a 401(k) plan," then described thusly:

"The Treasury receives the wire transfer and takes that amount that's for the employee, and immediately puts it over to the private sector in a custodial bank which then immediately invests it in a dollar-priced money market fund, in which you as the employee have personal property rights even though at that moment it's not known who you are or how much you put in. By the way, this level we refer to as Level 1. Around June or July the following year, when the tax paid and the savings invested is reconciled to your name, you have units in this account, which add up to how much you put in plus an interest credit based on how much that account earned or all the accounts earned during that time period. Let's say it's $1,200. Those units now go down into what we call Level 2. Level 2 is three balanced funds, highly diversified portfolios invested in U.S. stocks, U.S. bonds, foreign stocks, foreign bonds, and cash. There would be five sleeves within each balanced fund, and the weighting of those sleeves would differ. One would be highly weighted toward equities, for younger folks. One would be highly weighted toward fixed income for older folks. The middle one might be weighted 60-40.

"You could choose any one of the three you want. You would be told that these were designed for age. This is critical, because in the 401(k) world the big cost driver is education. And can you imagine educating 155 [million] Americans on the difference between a large-cap stock, a small-cap stock, the coefficient of variation—you're never going to get anywhere. But there's something that every single American knows and that's his age. And so you say. 'This is for the young age, this is for the middle age, and this is for the old age.' You can choose any of the three that you want, but you would go into the one that is age-specific to you. This is called Level 2.

"After the system is up and running for three to four years, you have an option to go down to Level 3. Level 3 is a retail platform—mutual fund companies, registered investment advisers, insurance companies.

"By the way, your savings still go back up into Level 1, and it can drop down to Level 2, then Level 3, or directly from Level 1 to Level 3, if you wish. . . ."

Shipman is a sincere believer in the power of the markets, but as I listened to his tortured précis and tried to imagine how 155 million Americans might keep track of the levels and sleeves on which their retirement security depended, I realized that he had created a private account system that only a stockbroker could love.

Toward the end of the second day, Santorum, anointed to be one of the shepherds of Social Security reform on the Senate floor, stepped to the lectern to describe what might be called the content-free version of privatization.

"You hear a lot of people say the president isn't coming forward and saying how he's going to fix the whole system. I would argue the president does not need to come forward and do that. He came forward with something new, which is hope. That's really what personal retirement accounts are all about. They're about hope. Without the personal retirement account that hope is gone. It's as simple as that."

The session closed with one last triumphalist partisan outburst, a borderline paranoid tirade by Michael Barone, once a respected political analyst, now a familiar ranter on the Fox News Channel. Barone placed Social Security at the center of the culture war between left and right that has befouled American politics for nearly three decades. Opposition to private accounts arises from the Democrats' "hatred of George Bush," he said, with the "old media, the *New York Times,* ABC, CBS, NBC, the left-leaning old media . . . who did everything they could to defeat George W. Bush in the last election. They pulled out all the stops, used any tactics, including bogus stories, slanting of the news and so forth, and instead of defeating Bush they discredited themselves. We now have new media, talk radio, the Fox News Channel—number one in cable news—the blogosphere. . . ."

I emerged from Cato's headquarters with my head in a fog, trying to sort out fact from cant. I wondered if it could be true, as Barone had suggested so confidently, that the tide of American opinion was swinging inexorably away from traditional Social Security and the idea that society has a communal responsibility to care for the least fortunate among us, and that George Bush's powers of persuasion were convincing the American public that Social Security was dead and that the only "hope," to use Santorum's word, was for each of us to look out only for ourselves.

Then I saw that morning's *USA Today*, featuring the latest nationwide Gallup Poll results. It reported that 55 percent of the poll sample considered private accounts coupled with a sharp cut in basic benefits—in other words, the Bush blueprint—a "bad idea." They favored by more than a 2-to-1 margin limiting benefits for wealthy retirees and raising the payroll tax ceiling. Only 30 percent believed that investing private accounts in stocks and bonds would yield them better retirement benefits than traditional Social Security, and 64 percent believed that their benefits would end up about the same or lower. Despite the president's remarkable powers of persuasion, the general opinion of privatization hadn't budged: people were against it.

When members of Congress returned to Washington in March from a midterm break in their home districts, the Republicans seemed shaken. Those who had faced voters at public forums had gotten an earful. They learned that the voters still trusted Social Security and mistrusted Wall Street. Most people weren't confident that investing in stocks and bonds would invariably reward them with untold wealth, as Bill Shipman and his friends at Cato assured them. They might be intrigued by the potential yields of private accounts, but they aren't at all prepared to sacrifice Social Security to get them.

More polls showed the public acceptance of privatization to be sinking, as was President Bush's credibility on the subject. The administration backpedaled gingerly. The president allowed that he might accept lifting the wage cap on the payroll tax to increase Social Security revenues as something short of a tax increase. Republican leaders in Congress began talking about debating reform for another year or two, rather than jamming a program through in a few months.

The first volley of shock and awe had drawn to a close, but it hadn't driven the program's supporters out of their bunkers. Not yet, anyway. The White House had money, it had compliant right-wing acolytes in the press, and it had the president's earnest self-assurance that the system would soon be "flat broke." The first round was over, but the enemies of Social Security were preparing for a long war.

On March, Treasury Secretary John Snow launched a taxpayer-financed website designed to "provide up-to-date information on the problems facing Social Security and the administration's efforts to permanently fix the program through bipartisan reform." The openly partisan StrengtheningSocialSecurity.gov featured a new "Fact of the Day" on its home page every day ("The President's proposals will not change the Social Security system in any way for those born before 1950," etc.). The only so-called solution mentioned anywhere on the site was the creation of private accounts. In a welcoming video, President Bush showed that he hadn't tempered his position at all on the future of Social Security or what he considered the most appropriate reform.

"Social Security was a great moral success of the *twentieth century*," he said, hitting the last two words hard to suggest that the program's time had passed. "For younger workers, the government has made promises it cannot keep. That means Social Security is set to go broke just when you reach retirement. . . ."

The familiar discreditable claims made their appearance: the threat of "bankruptcy," the certainty of "drastically higher taxes or massive new borrowing or sudden and severe cuts in Social Security benefits . . . if steps are not taken." Doggedly loyal to the end to his roster of fabricated facts and plain misinformation, Bush closed with an earnest observation. "If we approach the Social Security debate with courage and honesty," he said, "we can succeed."

Chapter Thirteen

What's Really Wrong
with Social Security
(and How to Fix It)

ONE OF THE BIG LIES told by the enemies of Social Security is that opponents of privatization don't wish to make any changes in the program—as though the only choice is between private accounts and no reform at all.

The truth is that even Social Security's most devoted advocates know that the system requires changes. Constant modification is characteristic of all defined-benefit plans; nobody can ever know in advance what variations in life expectancy, wages, interest rates, and dozens of other factors will occur to affect their fiscal balance. The many adjustments in benefits and tax rates that have been made to Social Security through the years aren't the result of flaws in the program, but reflections of its basic structure.

The program's founders knew that its rules and finances would never be static. Arthur Altmeyer, the system's first commissioner, called Social Security "a goal, never a finished thing, because human aspirations are infinitely expandable just as human nature is infinitely perfectible."

Defined-contribution plans such as private retirement accounts are no less sensitive to economic and financial vicissitudes: a crash in the stock market may mean a sharp decline in the value of the account; the death of a breadwinner will mean the end of the contribution stream. The difference is that the costs of these changes are borne by the plans' individual owners, not by the overall system. This is a drawback, because some individual plan owners may not have the financial resources to carry out the necessary adjustments.

Over the years, Congresses and presidents have made numerous changes in Social Security to respond not only to new economic realities but to demographic developments as well. It is time for another round. The question is not whether Social Security should be reformed, but what aspects of the program should be reformed, and how.

Thanks to the meticulous number crunching performed by parties interested in the Social Security debate, including the system's own actuaries, we can quantify how much reform is needed. The amount is equal to the system's long-term actuarial deficit, or the imbalance between the inflow and outflow of the system over a given period. As noted earlier, the conventional period used for most Social Security estimations is 75 years, because as a rough approximation of the lifespan of an American worker it's not too short to give us a reasonable understanding of the impact of a given program change, and not so long that we feel obligated to respond to conditions that are so far off in time that we can't really say that they'll ever occur.

As these words are written, the Social Security actuaries estimate the deficit over the 75 years ending in 2080 at 1.92 percent of taxable payroll. (This is based on the intermediate-case projection.) In other words, the deficit could be eliminated by raising current Social Security taxes by 1.92 percentage points to 14.32 percent of wages, by reducing benefits by an equivalent amount, or by a combination of the two.

Genuine reformers—those without the ulterior motives of changing the relationship between government and citizen or scoring a win for the conservative movement—should be seeking a combination that addresses the deficit's causes fairly and judiciously, yet does not violate Social Security's core principles.

The first task is to understand what causes the deficit. There are two major factors.

Improved life expectancy

The general life expectancy of Americans at age 65 has risen by about four and a half years since 1940. The average worker reaching 65 that year could expect to live until about age 79. By 2002 the average 65-year-old's life expectancy had risen to beyond age 83.

This affects Social Security in two related ways. First, it means that retirement stipends—which are, after all, lifetime benefits—are paid out for longer periods on average than they used to be. Moreover, inflation makes these benefits more costly the longer they are paid out, since beneficiaries receive a cost-of-living raise every year. For example, the average monthly benefit for new retirees in 1988 was $560; by 2005, or 17 years later, annual cost-of-living increases had raised the monthly stipend for those retirees still living to $953.

Whether life expectancies among the middle-aged and elderly will continue to rise at the same rate is a question on which even experts in the field disagree. Even if the rate slows, however, the impact of the increases already seen will continue to ripple through the Social Security balance sheet for decades to come.

Statistics on life expectancies, unsurprisingly, vary by gender, race, and other categories. In 2002, white women aged 65 had the longest average life expectancy, to age 84½, followed by African-American women (83), white men (81½), and African-American men (79½).

The lag in life expectancy of black men has given rise to a mistaken notion that Social Security discriminates against African Americans. This misconception was fuel by a flawed and partisan 1998 analysis by the libertarian Heritage Foundation. The paper suggested that private accounts would be an advantage for African Americans, because their relatively short life expectancies lower their rates of return from Social Security payroll taxes.

The study's many critics—including the Social Security Administration—noted, however, that this conclusion fails to account for the fact that the lower average wages of African-American workers mean that they receive higher retirement benefits relative to their payroll contributions. More important, by focusing narrowly on old-age benefits, the study overlooked the fact that African-American workers and their families rely much more heavily than other ethnic groups on Social Security disability and dependent benefits. When these factors are accounted for, the rate of return on payroll tax contributions of lower-earning

African Americans can be as much as double that of average or high-earning white workers.

The longevity statistics do hint at a somewhat different inequity: Longer life expectancies tend to be concentrated at the high end of the earnings trendline. High wage earners live longer on average than their low-earning counterparts, and the gap is widening. This magnifies the effect that improvements in life expectancy have on Social Security's finances, because the workers who live longer receive the largest benefits in dollar terms. Additionally, as Peter A. Diamond and Peter R. Orszag have noted, the trend reduces the traditional lifetime progressivity of Social Security, because wealthier retirees tend to collect benefits for longer periods than lower-paid workers.

Any prudent reform of Social Security, therefore, should address the growing disparity in lifetime benefit patterns.

Disproportionate earnings growth

The share of total U.S. wage earnings that exceed the maximum wage subject to the payroll tax has soared since 1983, despite annual increases in the ceiling ($90,000 in 2005). The percentage of untaxed wages, which had reached 16 percent in the late 1970s, was lowered to 10 percent by the 1983 reforms drafted by the Greenspan commission. The commission presumably expected annual increases in the ceiling to hold the percentage steady, but that was not to be. By 2002, some 15 percent of all U.S. wages were exempt from the payroll tax, and the share has continued to rise.

This doesn't mean that the percentage of *workers* with earnings above the ceiling is rising. On the contrary, that ratio has remained fairly steady at about 6 percent since the 1983 reforms. What has happened is that the rich have gotten richer—the fortunate 6 percent have increased their share of tax-exempt wages to 15 percent from 10 percent. In effect, their payroll tax rate has fallen in relation to that of all other workers. This group also collects a disproportionate share of unearned income such as dividends, interest, and capital gains, which are entirely exempt from the payroll tax. To add insult to injury, they also received the lion's share of Bush administration tax cuts.

Because of these trends, the payroll tax has become more regressive since 1983, costing lower-paid workers much more than higher-paid workers when calculated as a share of their overall income. The Social Security program, accordingly, is being deprived of its claim on a progressively greater share of the national wealth. Any responsible reform should address the imbalance.

Since 1940, changes in the American workforce and family structure have thrown other aspects of Social Security out of whack. These include the system's treatment of divorced spouses and immigrants.

Under current law, divorced spouses of either sex are entitled to spousal and survivor benefits if their marriage lasted at least ten years. As the divorce rate in the United States has climbed, however, the length of the average marriage has fallen to fewer than eight years, leaving many divorced spouses without a Social Security claim. This may help explain the high poverty rate among elderly divorcées. Lowering the threshold to allow more divorced spouses to receive spousal and survivor benefits would be a simple, relatively inexpensive, and effective way to rectify the situation.

Immigration, particularly illegal immigration, presents a more complicated problem. Political rhetoric demonizing illegal immigrants has led the public to believe that they contribute almost nothing in labor or taxes while consuming a disproportionate share of public services. In fact, the 9 million illegal immigrants in the country are a crucial, if ill-paid, source of labor. Many pay Social Security taxes without any hope of collecting benefits, because they supply bogus Social Security numbers to legitimate (if not always unwitting) employers. Others are employed in jobs that are nominally covered by Social Security, but because of their dubious legal status they are paid under the table. This subterfuge deprives the system of contributions by the workers and their employers and further cheats the laborers of all the benefits of gainful employment in the United States.

Demographic projections suggest that as the native-born workforce shrinks, immigrant labor is going to become more important to the U.S. economy in coming years. The Social Security actuaries acknowledge this possibility in their best-case scenario, which forecasts that an influx of as many as 1.4 million immigrants a year—550,000 of them illegal—would help the system remain solvent indefinitely, even without tax increases or benefit reductions. Those figures are fairly close to current official estimates of immigration trends. The trustees' intermediate-case scenario, however, sets the influx of illegal immigrants at as low as 300,000 a year through 2080, or 200,000 fewer than the government says have arrived annually over the last 15 years.

A legislative solution to the issue of illegal immigrants is obviously beyond the scope of this book. But there is little room for doubt that acknowledging their role in the U.S. economy and regularizing their legal status would expand the pool of wage earners and wages subject to the payroll tax. This would almost surely produce net positive consequences for Social Security (not to mention for the immigrants themselves).

Our survey of prudent reforms for Social Security begins with a look at some oft-mentioned nostrums that will have a more deleterious effect on the program than their supporters acknowledge. Here are three to avoid.

Converting Social Security to a means-tested program

Advocates of means testing—paying benefits only to those who fall below a certain annual income threshold—contend that the system spends too much on benefits to well-off people who don't need money.

Their goal is to convert Social Security into the equivalent of a welfare program. Misreading the historical record, they often say that this was the original intention of the program's founders. (The Social Security system already administers a welfare program for the elderly—Supplemental Security Income, or SSI, which provides benefits based not on the recipient's work history but entirely on the basis of need.)

The truth is that the drafters of the Social Security Act explicitly rejected the use of a means test to limit basic benefits. Forcing people to assert their poverty before receiving benefits was a demeaning process they were determined to avoid. Instead, they designed a system in which payments would be tied, if loosely, to each worker's career earnings, and in which every wage earner would receive something.

Means testing would lead to Social Security's demise. The program's universality has been a key to its survival through numerous turns of the political screw during the last 70 years. As

Franklin D. Roosevelt anticipated, its "ownership" by millions of workers and beneficiaries has always discouraged previous attempts to dismantle or privatize the system. Means-tested welfare programs have not fared so well. Lacking broad political support, they are often the first programs on the chopping block when state and federal budgets come under pressure. Their beneficiaries are often stigmatized as lazy and undeserving.

One alternative to means testing as a way of reducing benefits for the well-to-do is already in place: Social Security benefits paid to people with significant personal means—$25,000 in annual income for single taxpayers and $32,000 for couples filing jointly—are subject to limited income tax. (The Treasury allocates the revenues from the tax to Social Security and the Medicare program.)

Many regard this tax as a sort of back-door means test. That's true only to the extent that it shifts benefits toward the lower end of the income scale. But it's fundamentally different in that it preserves the tradition of universality that has helped sustain the program's popularity.

Indexing initial benefits to increases in prices, not wages

This deceptively simple-sounding change is also popular among privateers. The 2001 Bush Commission to Strengthen Social Security made it a central element in its master plan. Fans of this reform argue that wage indexing is a major driver of Social Security costs, which is true; and that it ensures that Social Security will remain insolvent regardless of the level of overall economic growth, which is untrue. They say that adjusting initial benefits to keep pace with inflation alone—a smaller adjustment—should be sufficient to enable retirees to keep up with economic changes.

Wage indexing means that every retiree's initial benefit is set according to a formula based on his or her highest 35 years of earnings, multiplied by a factor based on the average overall wage growth over much of that period. Once the initial benefit is established, it continues to be adjusted for inflation via an annual cost-of-living raise.

Social Security's critics argue that wage indexing gives future retirees entirely undeserved increases in benefits over and above inflation. As White House aide Peter Wehner remarked in his infamous memo to the conservative faithful: "No one on this planet can tell you why a 25-year-old person today is entitled [in 2050] to a 40 percent increase in Social Security benefits (in real terms) compared to what a person retiring today receives."

Perhaps Mr. Wehner simply wasn't listening very closely. The rationale for wage indexing has been well understood for many decades: it's that the standard of living is related to overall economic growth, which correlates closely in turn with wage growth—not price growth. Indeed, wages tend to grow faster than inflation by an average of about 1 percent a year. (Wehner understood that part of the phenomenon—that's why he projected that today's 25-year-olds would be collecting an inflation-adjusted benefit four decades from now that would be 40 percent higher than today's.) By raising benefits in sync with overall economic growth, in other words, wage indexing ensures that workers do not suffer a sharp drop in their standard of living upon retirement.

Automatic wage indexing of initial benefits began in the 1970s, when Congress relinquished the chore of manually reset-

ting benefit levels every couple of years. But the idea that benefits should keep pace with overall wage growth was implicit in
Social Security before then; Congress always took into account
economic growth, as well as inflation, every time it adjusted benefits prior to the 1970s. The effectiveness of its adjustments is evident from the fact that the so-called replacement level, the
median percentage of a worker's final wage that is replaced by
his or her initial Social Security benefit, has remained fairly
steady, in the range of 40 to 45 percent, since 1940.

Were benefits indexed to prices instead of wages, they would
gradually decline as a percentage of workers' final earnings.
Eventually the replacement level would be so insignificant that
the program would simply fade away.

Diverting payroll tax revenues to fund private accounts

The shortcomings of this proposal have occupied much of our
discussion. Carving out private accounts from Social Security's
existing funding stream will make the system financially less
stable, not stronger. It will shift the risk of economic and market
cycles from society to individuals, moreover, tearing a gaping
hole in the social safety net.

Many opportunities for workers to make tax-advantaged investments for their own retirements already exist—including
IRAs, Roth IRAs, Keogh plans, and 401(k) plans. Most wage
earners don't take advantage of these plans at all, and of those
who do, most don't make the maximum permissible annual contributions. That suggests that a better way to satisfy the public's
craving for individually managed retirement accounts—if there

is such a craving, which is arguable—is to add incentives for workers to exploit the opportunities Congress has already provided. We will examine some ideas in the next section.

Now that we have dispensed with reforms to avoid, we can turn our attention to several that are crucial.

Adjust benefits to changes in life expectancy

Considering the heavy strain placed on the system by the increased longevity of Americans reaching the age of 65, some accommodation to this actuarial trend is necessary and inevitable.

The most common proposal is to raise the normal retirement age, at which a worker becomes entitled to full Social Security benefits. This approach was taken by Congress in implementing the recommendations of the 1983 Greenspan commission. The 1983 reforms called for gradually raising the retirement age from 65 to 67 over the following 40 years. Later amendments slightly stretched out the process, so that the normal retirement age is currently scheduled to rise to 67 for retirees born in 1960 or later.

Speeding up the increase and raising the target age to 68 would improve the actuarial balance by 0.52 percent of covered payroll, according to the Social Security actuaries. Raising the target to 70 would yield 0.68 percent of covered payroll. This change, then, could reduce the 75-year deficit, currently calculated by the Social Security actuaries at 1.92 percent of covered payroll, by roughly one-fourth to one-third.

A different approach has been suggested by Peter Diamond and Peter Orszag. To avoid the inequity that raising the retirement age might impose on workers in stressful or physically taxing jobs, they propose leaving the normal retirement age at 65, but anually adjusting initial benefits and taxes by a factor related to recent improvements in life expectancy instead. Their plan would reduce the deficit by 0.55 percent of taxable payroll.

Each approach tries to balance the longer average periods over which today's workers collect benefits by reducing monthly stipends, with the goal of keeping the average lifetime benefit stable. The Diamond-Orszag plan does so directly; raising the retirement age does so by requiring those who still wish to retire at 65 or earlier to accept lower monthly payments. The pros and cons of each approach can be left to Congress, but either would preserve Social Security's basic structure.

Spread the burden of the legacy debt more broadly

One aspect of Social Security that all Americans share is its past—the debt bequeathed by the decision to award the first cohorts of retirees larger pensions than their contributions warranted. This was the "greatest generation" of popular legend, the Americans who carried the country through the Great Depression and two world wars. Even if one desires to question this generous policy today, it cannot be undone. The legacy debt belongs to us all.

Those who don't contribute to the program, or whose contributions are capped, arguably shoulder less than their fair share of their burden. They include state and local employees, who are the last major group of workers still largely exempt from membership in Social Security, and those whose wages exceed the payroll tax ceiling.

As Diamond and Orszag observe, state and local government

employees generally earn good wages. "It therefore seems appropriate that they pay their fair share, along with other higher earners, of Social Security's redistributive cost . . . as well as the cost of more generous benefits to earlier cohorts." Enrolling newly hired state and local workers in Social Security would immediately reduce the actuarial deficit by 0.21 percent, according to the Social Security actuaries. That's because the workers will begin paying payroll taxes long before they start retiring in significant numbers. As more of them retire, this positive impact will dwindle and eventually disappear; the actuaries calculate that by 2080 the new workers' impact on the system's balance of payments will be effectively zero.

Eliminating the payroll tax ceiling, however, would have a huge and lasting effect on the deficit. The Social Security actuaries calculate that abolishing the limit while retaining the existing cap on benefits would produce a gain of 2.2 percent of covered payroll—enough to completely close the 75-year deficit, with some money left over. (The actuaries' intermediate-case projection does indicate, however, that the deficit would reemerge at some point beyond the 75-year horizon.)

The actuaries also calculated the impact of a more limited tax increase on higher-earning workers, namely raising the ceiling to a point where it again covers 90 percent of the nation's aggregate wages rather than the current ratio of less than 85 percent. That change would reduce the deficit by 0.75 percent of payroll, or by more than one-third.

The idea of raising payroll tax revenues by hoisting the cap has recently gained some traction in Washington. In February, President Bush signaled his willingness to consider the change, which he plainly regards as preferable to raising the overall payroll tax rate above the current 12.4 percent.

Numerous ideas for adjusting the wage ceiling have been floated by Social Security reformers over the years; all are attempts to balance the need for new revenue with the realities of politics. These include proposals to tax earnings above a given cap at a reduced rate or to couple a raise in the tax ceiling with a raise in the maximum retirement benefit. Most proposals would significantly reduce the long-term deficit.

Allow the trust fund to invest in corporate equities

This idea was formally proposed by Robert Ball during the advisory council deliberations of 1994–1996 and was later endorsed by President Clinton. The most common variant would permit the trustees to invest up to 40 percent of the trust fund assets, which are currently restricted to special-issue U.S. government bonds, in corporate stocks.

This reform would allow the program to capture some of the potentially greater investment yields of equities without exposing individual beneficiaries to the very real risks of investing in the stock market. As Diamond and Orszag point out, investing through the trust fund would also allow the costs of severe market reversals to be spread across generations, instead of concentrating them among those cohorts with the unfortunate timing to be invested in stocks when a downdraft arrived. Centralizing the system's equity investments through the multi-billion-dollar trust fund, instead of making them via tens of millions of individual accounts, would also prevent transaction fees and other costs from eating into the returns.

Objections to allowing Social Security to invest outside the government securities market were first heard in 1935, when lawmakers quailed at the potential for conflicts of interest and political meddling if the federal government were to cast its long shadow into the corporate boardroom. Years of experience in government-sponsored equity investing—through state pension boards and the federal government's own Thrift Savings Plan, among other things—should put those fears to rest. Experience suggests that the key to trouble-free public investing is to place the funds under the control of an indisputably independent investment board with clear instructions to manage for maximum returns and to ignore all other considerations, including social and political pressure. Further restrictions might be imposed on the board's freedom to vote on shareholder or management resolutions, possibly by requiring the board to cast its votes in the same proportion as all other shareholders, or simply to abstain on all shareholder matters. Many brokerages holding shares in client accounts follow similar rules whenever they have not received specific instructions from the individual shareowners.

The Social Security actuaries, reluctant to commit themselves to a forecast for the stock market's performance over the next 75 years, calculated the potential gains from this change under three scenarios. Assuming that equities return an average 6.5 percent a year after inflation, they estimated that investing 40 percent of the trust fund in equities would reduce the system's deficit by 0.91 percent of payroll, or by nearly half. Assuming a return of 5.5 percent after inflation, the reduction would be 0.66 percent, or about one-third of the deficit. Assuming an after-inflation return of 3 percent—the standard risk-adjusted return matching the yields of the government bonds in the trust fund—the effect would be, naturally, zero.

If one assumes that aggregate returns from U.S. equities are certain to outrace inflation, as privatization advocates contend, then the most prudent, safest, and most inexpensive method of capturing those returns for Social Security is certainly to allow the trust fund in to the stock market.

Many observers have noted that broadening the system's investment options would have one other salutary effect: trust fund assets that were invested in private equities would be sequestered outside the federal Treasury, unlike the system's holdings of government securities. They would consequently be better protected from what Senator Moynihan labled the "thievery" of presidents and Congress.

Taken together, these three important reforms—correlating benefits to longer life expectancies, spreading the legacy debt more broadly, and expanding the trust fund's investment options—would eliminate Social Security's actuarial deficit for the next 75 years. The system would not be rendered sound forever, but a permanent fix is neither a necessary standard for reform nor a desirable one. Later generations will insist on the flexibility to design their own version of Social Security, as have past generations.

That doesn't exhaust the list of desirable reforms, however. Many other changes are worth considering, whether to redress inequities in the structure of benefits, or to spread the cost of this effective and indispensable program more fairly among all sectors of society. High on the list are these proposals.

Improve benefits for surviving spouses

One social group whose economic status has been largely unaffected by Social Security is aged widows, whose poverty rate is about four times that of elderly couples. (Although survivor benefits are paid by the gender-neutral Social Security system to widows or widowers, widows still suffer most from the decline in family income that accompanies the death of a spouse.)

One reason for this group's plight is that Social Security survivor benefits can fall below those of a married couple by 50 percent or more. This results from the structure of couples' benefits. Social Security pays one-earner couples a joint retirement stipend equal to 150 percent of what the working spouse would receive as a single person. For two-earner couples, the rule is slightly more complicated. The lower-paid spouse can choose to receive either the benefits due on his or her own account, or the joint benefit of 150 percent based on the higher-earning partner's record. Obviously, a couple would be likely to choose the joint benefit if the lower-paid spouse's retirement benefits on his or her own would be less than half that of the better-paid partner.

If both partners opt to receive their individual benefits, then the surviving spouse retains only his or her benefit after the partner's death. This could mean a drop in income of 50 percent or more, depending on whether the higher- or lower-earning spouse is the survivor. Under the second option, the survivor receives 100 percent of the higher-earning spouse's benefit—which translates into a one-third drop in the survivor's Social Security income.

Either eventuality can produce economic hardship for the survivor; many studies suggest that the cost of living for a surviving spouse is as much as 80 percent that of a couple. Therefore, it's reasonable to alleviate the income jolt that can occur after a spouse's death; a common proposal is to raise the survivor's benefit to 75 percent of the joint stipend.

Encourage employees to fund tax-advantaged retirement plans outside of Social Security

The government spent $85 billion on tax incentives for voluntary defined contribution plans in 2001, the largest such expenditure in the federal budget. Most of this subsidy was paid to wealthier taxpayers, whose enrollment rates in tax-advantaged programs such as 401(k) plans and individual retirement accounts are much higher than lower-earning workers. Even those lower-wage workers who do enroll in such programs tend not to contribute the maximum amount; in the case of 401(k) plans, this means they often fail to take full advantage of employers' matching contributions.

"Virtually every company offering a 401(k) plan has employees who aren't taking full advantage of their 401(k) plan and aren't contributing enough to get the full company match— which means they are essentially leaving free money on the table," observes a study by Hewitt Associates, a human resources consulting firm, analyzing why many workers don't adequately save for retirement.

Increased tax incentives or higher contribution limits would probably achieve little, beyond delivering an even greater subsidy to well-heeled workers who don't need it. But changing federal law to mandate that all new employees be automatically enrolled in their employers' 401(k) plans unless they opt out could double enrollment rates in the target population, according to several studies.

Increasing the take-up rate of private pension plans by lower-paid workers would not in itself relieve Social Security's fiscal condition. But it would help reduce the overreliance of many workers on Social Security for all their retirement income. The program's original function, after all, was to be one of three pillars of a comfortable retirement—supplemented by employer-sponsored pensions and personal savings.

Roll back the recent tax cuts

Despite the Bush administration's contention that the long-term deficit will make Social Security unaffordable, barring dramatic changes to the system, the program's shortfall pales in comparison to the cost of the president's tax policy. If the tax cuts enacted at his behest from 2001 through 2003 are made permanent, as he proposes, they will cost 1.95 percent of gross domestic product over the next 75 years, or $11.6 trillion in present value. That's almost three times as much as the Social Security shortfall, which would come to only 0.65 percent of GDP over the same period, or $4 trillion in present value.

Indeed, the present value of the president's tax cuts over the next 75 years alone is more than the present value of the Social Security deficit calculated to *infinity* (a mere $11 trillion). This should give perspective to the White House's claim that Social Security is on an "unsustainable" course.

These figures point to an obvious trade-off: even a one-third rollback of the tax cuts—more than half of which went to taxpayers with income of more than $100,000—would produce enough revenue to close the 75-year deficit completely.

Some reformers have toyed with the idea of directing specific federal tax revenues to Social Security. One good candidate for such a role is the estate tax, which the Bush administration proposes to abolish after 2010. That year, the tax rate would be 45 percent, subject to an exemption of $3.5 million per person. At such a level the tax would apply only to the largest one-half of one percent of the nation's estates. Diamond and Orszag, who have proposed retaining the tax in its 2010 form instead of abolishing it, calculate that applying the revenues to Social Security would pay for as much as one-fifth of the 75-year actuarial deficit. Their proposal even echoes the grassroots reform movements of the 1930s that helped inspire Social Security: Huey Long, Dr. Townsend, and Upton Sinclair all shared a desire to raise a fair share of government revenues from inherited wealth.

Consider other adjustments to benefits and revenues

The breadth of Social Security and the complex mechanisms that transform contributions into benefits leave much room for modest adjustments that can have significant positive effects on the system's financial stability.

On the benefit side, several reform proposals target the annual cost-of-living raise, which is currently keyed to the consumer price index compiled by the U.S. Department of Labor. Many economists maintain that the CPI consistently overstates the impact of inflation by about 0.22 percent a year. That's because it doesn't account for the so-called substitution effect, through which consumers react to price increases in certain products by purchasing lower-priced variants. Reducing the annual cost-of-living raise by an average 0.5 percent would eliminate as much as 42 percent of the long-term deficit, arguably without imposing a significant burden on beneficiaries.

Another way to cut benefits modestly is to increase the number of work years used in the formula for calculating average lifetime earnings. Currently, Social Security computes basic benefits from an average of the worker's 35 highest-earning years. Factoring in three more low-earning years would tend to decrease average overall benefits by about 3 percent. This change would decrease the long-term deficit by more than 40 percent, according to actuarial projections. It would, however, have a disproportionate effect on workers with shorter careers or with lengthy periods of unemployment, including stay-at-home parents.

On the revenue side, one proposal to raise the program's income would apply the same taxation rules to Social Security benefits as are applied to private pensions. Under current law, pensions derived from pre-tax contributions, including most 401(k) payouts, are taxed as ordinary income; those derived from after-tax income are not. The underlying principle is that all income should be taxed only once, either when it is withdrawn from a tax-deferred account or when it is contributed to a taxable account.

If this principle were applied to Social Security benefits, then the portion of a retirement check that derives from the worker's half share of the payroll tax would be exempt from income tax. The portion of retirement benefits derived from the employer's half of the payroll tax, and any benefits paid over and above the worker's contributions, would be fully taxable in the year they are received.

Some experts have calculated that this change would require 85 percent of all benefits to be declared as taxable income. But lower-income recipients would gain a relative advantage, for their income tax rate would still be at the low end of the scale. The change would reduce the long-term deficit by about one-fifth.

*   *   *

The point of mentioning these proposals is not to endorse any of them specifically, but simply to illustrate the variety of approaches available to address Social Security's financial issues.

The reform proposals covered in this chapter have several features in common. They recognize that Social Security has imperfections that require redress, whether for the sake of equity or for fiscal prudence. They all strive to strengthen the system while preserving the fundamental characteristics of social insurance and upholding the program's role as a bridge between generations and among Americans in each generation. They honor Social Security's unexampled success in eradicating poverty among large segments of the American community.

Of course, if one wishes to solve Social Security's manifold problems without regard to how retirees and disabled workers and their families will fare as a consequence, the obvious course is to shut the program down.

This is the essence of the plot against Social Security: dismantling the program under the guise of providing what President Bush calls a "permanent fix."

The president's desire to replace the communal responsibility that Social Security implies with the "ownership society," which glorifies personal responsibility and disparages big government, may sound reasonable—until one remembers that Americans once lived in such a free-market paradise.

It was the 1920s, and it ended with an economic catastrophe that gave birth to the very program Bush is plotting to dismantle. The truly pressing issue for Social Security is not how to protect it from the inevitable uncertainties of the economy and demographics of tomorrow, but how to protect it from those who would destroy it today.

Notes

Chapter 1: The Bush Blitz

5 *business and government*   Hacker in Peter Gosselin, "If America Is Richer, Why Are Its Families So Much Less Secure?" *Los Angeles Times,* October 10, 2004.

6 *Such a policy*   Robert J. Schiller, "American Casino: The Promise and Perils of Bush's 'Ownership Society,'" *Atlantic Monthly,* March 2005.

10 *a vocal minority*   Remarks at a forum sponsored by the National Committee to Preserve Social Security and Medicare, Washington, D.C., January 13, 2005.

11 *It is a good bet*   Richard C. Leone in H. J. Aaron and R. D. Reischauer, *Countdown to Reform: The Great Social Security Debate,* p. vii.

12 *It should be plain*   Ibid.

12 *easily forgotten*   Jeff Madrick, "Social Security and Its Discontents," in *New York Review of Books,* December 19, 1996.

15 *2005 surplus*   Figures are from the 2004 report of the Social Security trustees.

17 *by far the largest*   Austan Goolsbee, "The Fees of Private Accounts and the Impact of Social Security Privatization on Financial Managers," University of Chicago Graduate School of Business, September 2004, at http://gsb.uchicago.edu/pdf/ssec_goolsbee.pdf.

17 *No wonder*   Stuart Butler and Peter Germanis, "Achieving a 'Leninist' Strategy," *Cato Journal,* vol.3, no. 2 (Fall 1983), p. 548.

18 *guerrilla warfare*   Butler and Germanis, p. 552.

19 *editorialists at the* Wall Street Journal   See, for example, Lindley H. Clark Jr., "Speaking of Business," *Wall Street Journal,* July 24, 1984.

NOTES

19 A *"flagship"*   Lawrence R. Jacobs and Robert Y. Shapiro, "Myths and Misunderstandings about Public Opinion toward Social Security," in R. D. Arnold, M. Graetz, and A. H. Munnell (eds.): *Framing the Social Security Debate: Values, Politics, and Economics,* p. 364.

20 *You know*   George J. Church and Richard Lacayo, "Social Insecurity," *Time,* March 20, 1995.

20 *When a similar*   Jacobs and Shapiro, p. 364.

20 *Most important*   Ibid.

20 *A series of polls*   Jacobs and Shapiro, p. 365.

21 *There is a firm coalition*   Butler and Germanis, p. 548.

21 *Instead of spreading*   Ibid., p. 549.

22 *ugly intergenerational conflict*   James Tobin, "The Future of Social Security: One Economist's Assessment," Cowles Foundation Discussion Paper No. 820, February 1987, p. 9.

23 *"substitution" effect*   M. Feldstein (ed.), *Privatizing Social Security,* p. 11.

23 *This may be true*   Roger Lowenstein, "A Question of Numbers," *New York Times Magazine,* January 16, 2005.

Chapter 2: The Cornerstone

25 *gagged*   Kenneth S. Davis, *FDR: The New Deal Years, 1933–1937,* p. 459.

26 *kiss of death*   Barbara Armstrong, quoted by Davis, p. 454.

27 *Unemployment had peaked*   Sylvester J. Schieber and John R. Shoven, *The Real Deal: The History and Future of Social Security,* p. 21.

27 *Among men over 65*   Schieber and Shoven, p. 22.

27 *The proportion of Americans*   Arthur M. Schlesinger Jr., *The Age of Roosevelt: The Politics of Upheaval,* p. 29.

27 *They had spent their lives*   Ibid.

28 *She is helpless*   The letter is posted on the Social Security Administration's history page, at www.ssa.gov/history/lettertoFDR.html.

28 *The world's first national*   Schieber and Shoven, p. 17.

29 *44 states had launched*   Ibid., p. 18.

30 *"Three haggard, very old women"*   quoted in Schlesinger, p. 30.

31 *More than 5,000 Townsend Clubs*   Davis, p. 402.

31 *the first effective pressure group*   Ibid.

31 *Onward, Townsend*   Schlesinger, p. 34.

32 *hillbilly's paradise*   Ibid., p. 63.

33 *It is symptoms*   Ibid., p.65.

33 *Sinclair proposed that the state* This description of EPIC is drawn from Davis, pp. 403–4.

34 *even enlisting Hollywood* Schlesinger, p. 119.

35 *some safeguard* The message is quoted in Schieber and Shoven, p. 27.

35 *Putting the elderly* Schieber and Shoven, p. 33.

36 *the same old dole* Davis, p. 460.

36 *The alternative* Ibid., p. 456.

38 *The Founders* Dorcas Hardy and C. Colburn Hardy, *Social Insecurity,* p. 5.

38 *had the least economic security* Davis, p. 460.

38 *on the usual grounds* Davis, p. 461.

39 *astonishingly inept* William E. Leuchtenburg, *Franklin D. Roosevelt and the New Deal,* p. 132.

39 *historic assumptions* Ibid., p. 133.

40 *desperately in search* Davis, p. 643.

40 *The Republican Party* Schlesinger, p. 614; Schieber and Shoven, p. 53.

40 *ruthlessly disregardful* Davis, p. 643.

41 *compelled by a Roosevelt* Ibid.

41 *Republican National Committee* Schieber and Shoven, p. 53.

41 *You're sentenced* Ibid.

41 *On the very eve* Schlesinger, p. 636.

41 *Having decided* Altmeyer, Arthur J. Oral History #4, at http://www.ssa.gov/history/ajaoral.html.

42 *Only desperate men* Davis, pp. 644–45.

42 *He later called* Ibid., p. 643.

Chapter 3: The Legacy of Ida May Fuller

44 *It wasn't that I expected* "The First Social Security beneficiary," at http://www.ssa.gov/history/imf.html.

45 *Younger workers should remember* Edward M. Gramlich, "Social Security Reform in the Twenty-first Century," April 19, 2001, at www.federalreserve.gov/boarddocs/speeches/2001.

46 *All those born* Peter A. Diamond and Peter R. Orszag, *Saving Social Security: A Balanced Approach,* p. 71.

46 *As the economists* Ibid.

47 Aaron and Reischauer, p. 59.

47 *To illustrate* This illustration is adapted from Diamond and Orszag, pp. 6–7.

49 *Robert M. Ball*   Schieber and Shoven, p. 289.

50 *starve and die*   Tobin, p. 20.

50 *two oft-proposed reforms*   Diamond and Orszag, pp. 88–90.

51 *a pay-as-you-go retirement system*   "How Pension Financing Affects Returns to Different Generations," *Long-Range Fiscal Policy Brief,* No. 12, September 22, 2004, Congressional Budget Office.

53 *Retirees would get roughly the same*   Geanakoplos et al., in Arnold, Graetz, and Munnell (eds.), p. 148.

53 *whether this is a tradeoff*   Ibid., p. 150.

Chapter 4: The Assumption Game

58 *significant uncertainty*   S. C. Goss, A. H. Wade, and J. P. Schultz, Actuarial Note 2004.1, *Unfunded Obligation and Transition Cost for the OASDI,* August 2004, Social Security Administration.

58 *fertility, mortality*   2004 Annual Report of the Social Security Trustees, p. 70.

64 *Before that*   Robinson, personal communication with author, February 8, 2005.

66 *Not many mortals*   PriceWaterhouseCoopers Report on Actuarial Projection of the Social Security Trust Funds, General Accounting Office, January 14, 2000, p. 22.

68 *The trustees justified*   See, for example, the 2003 annual report of the trustees, p. 97.

68 *somewhat incredibly*   Gordon, "Exploding Productivity Growth: Context, Causes, and Implications" in Brookings Papers on Economic Activity, 2:2003, p. 267.

72 *Sean Tuffnell*   Sean Tuffnell, "Kerry's Secret Social Security Plan—Revealed!" National Review Online, July 29, 2004, at http://www.nationalreview.com/nrof_comment/tuffnell200407290914.asp.

Chapter 5: The Reagan Revolution Meets the Baby Boom

74 *high-water mark*   Schieber and Shoven, p. 165.

74 *Samuelson*   Newsweek, February 12, 1967, quoted in Schieber and Shoven, p. 110.

75 *growing up was a lot easier*   Tobin, p. 11.

77 *A 20 percent increase*   quoted in Edward D. Berkowitz, *Robert Ball and the Politics of Social Security,* pp. 205–6.

77 *wages grow faster*   Tobin, p. 13.

78 *no forecast*   Schieber and Shoven, p. 173.

79 *Americans had been deceived*   Ronald Reagan, *An American Life,* p. 140.

80 *Chicago welfare queen*   Lou Cannon, *President Reagan: The Role of a Lifetime,* pp. 456–57.

80 *Democratic accusations*   Reagan, p. 131.

81 *the very inner fortress*   David A. Stockman, *The Triumph of Politics,* p. 181.

82 *true heavy lifting*   Ibid., p. 125.

83 *Stockman buried*   Ibid., p. 187.

84 *Only sixty minutes*   Ibid.

84 *his eyes glazed*   Cannon, p. 212.

84 *You'll be the first*   Stockman, p. 188; Cannon, p. 212.

84 *hadn't thought through*   Stockman, p. 190.

84 *Tip O'Neill*   Schieber and Shoven, p. 188.

85 *Niskanen*   quoted in Cannon, p. 213.

85 *any major assault*   Ibid., p. 214.

85 *fobbed off*   Stockman, p. 332.

88 *"best-case" projection*   Schieber and Shoven, p. 191.

88 *The concept was presented to the panel*   Berkowitz, pp. 303–4.

89 *The commission's regular monthly meeting*   Ibid., p. 306.

89 *Meeting which never took place*   Berkowitz, p. 421.

89 *Powerful figures in the administration*   Ibid., pp. 307–8.

90 *Between 1990 and 2010*   Schieber and Shoven, p. 193.

91 *At the signing ceremony*   Schieber and Shoven, p. 195.

Chapter 6: The Myth of the Mythical Trust Fund

96 *No lockbox*   Charles Krauthammer, "2042: A Fiscal Odyssey," *Washington Post,* February 18, 2005.

96 *A shell game*   Hardy and Hardy, *Social Insecurity,* p. 22.

96 *At a meeting of corporate leaders*   Glenn Kessler, "O'Neill Faults 'No Assets' Social Security, *Washington Post,* June 19, 2001.

97 *contains no genuine assets*   Daniel J. Mitchell, "The Social Security Trust Fund Fraud," in *The Heritage Foundation Backgrounder* No. 1256, February 22, 1999. (Emphasis added.)

98 *neither Social Security*   Aaron and Reischauer, p. 52.

100 *too fantastic to comprehend*   Shieber and Shoven, p. 50.

100 *federal government undertaking*   Ibid., p. 69.

102 *That would be socialism*   Ibid., p. 70.

102 *social undertakings such as*   Ibid., p. 70.

103 *Social Security was widely perceived*   Ibid., p. 91.

103 *The law no longer*   Ibid., p. 181.

105 *1999 State of the Union*   Ibid., p. 348.

107 *Those bonds*   Thomas Sowell, "Social Security 'Trust Fund,'" *Capitalism* magazine, October 29, 2001. Available at www.capmag.com.

108 *the savings*   Schieber and Shoven, p. 203.

Chapter 7: Reform Comes Unstuck

113 *we did better*   "Oral History Collection: Robert M. Ball, Interview #6," October 25, 2001, Social Security Online, at www.ssa.gov/history/orals/ball6.html.

114 *protecting the sanctity*   Allen W. Smith, *The Looting of Social Security*, p. 87.

119 *They really didn't know*   Berkowitz, p. 346.

119 *Ball didn't think highly*   Ball, interview with author, January 29, 2005.

120 *hopelessly divided*   Schieber and Shoven, p. 263.

120 *Ball gave up early*   Berkowitz, p. 347.

121 *Chinese menu*   Schieber and Shoven, p. 271.

122 *stalking horse*   Berkowitz, p. 352.

122 *Like Scheiber's proposal*   Ibid., pp. 305–6.

123 *Frankly, I knew*   Gramlich, comments in Arnold, Graetz, and Munnell (eds.), p. 424.

124 *might be more palatable*   Gramlich speech at Bryn Mawr, Pennsylvania, April 19, 2001, available at www.federalreserve.gov/boarddocs/speeches/2001.

Chapter 8: The Privateers

129 *Big employers fear*   Thomas B. Edsall, "Conservatives Join Forces for Bush Plans," *Washington Post,* February 13, 2005.

132 *Cigarette taxes*   Dan Morgan, "Think Tanks: Corporations' Quiet Weapon," *Washington Post,* January 29, 2000.

133 *Simply a vehicle*   Thomas B. Edsall, "New Ways to Harness Soft Money in Works," *Washington Post,* August 25, 2002, p. A01.

133 *veneer of "seniors" legitimacy*   "United Seniors Association: Hired Guns for PhRMA and Other Corporate Interests," Public Citizen Congress Watch, July 2002, at http://www.citizen.org/congress/campaign/special_interest/articles.cfm?ID=7999.

134 *The group ran afoul*   Quotes are from Decision No. CR1075, Docket No. C-02-061, Departmental Appeals Board, Dept. of Health and Human Services Administrative Law Judge Steven T.

Kessel, August 8, 2003.

135 *boulder in the middle*   Glenn Justice, "A New Target for Advisers to Swift Vets," *New York Times,* February 21, 2005.

136 *traditional community causes*   Dan Morgan, "Conservatives: A Well-Financed Network," *Washington Post,* January 4, 1981, p. A1.

137 *I find it hard*   Milton Friedman, "Speaking the Truth About Social Security Reform," *New York Times,* January 11, 1999.

139 *Into the void*   Joshua M. Marshall, "Privatization, Inc.," *American Prospect,* July 30, 2001.

140 *According to a report at the time*   Ibid.

140 *Invited as a keynote speaker*   Kessler, "O'Neill Faults 'No Assets' Social Security."

141 *Multimillion-dollar contributions*   "The Business Blitz on Security," *National Journal,* January 22, 2005.

141 *his grandfather would "surely oppose"*   Ibid.

142 *Max's group was dubbed*   "Wall Street Plays Reticent Over Plan for Privatizing," Tom Petruno and Walter Hamilton, *Los Angeles Times,* January 23, 2005.

142 *Most people in the business*   Ibid.

Chapter 9: The Ownership Scam 1

143 *the power of the market*   Milton Friedman and Rose D. Friedman, *Free to Choose,* p. 9.

144 *Pundits assured a rapt audience*   See James K. Glassman and Kevin A. Hassett, *Dow 36,000.*

144 *This isn't a game show*   Sam Beard, "Minimum-Wage Millionaires," *Policy Review,* Summer 1995.

145 *Risky investments*   Martin Feldstein (ed.), *Privatizing Social Security,* p. 247.

147 *Does a falling stock market*   Andrew G. Biggs, "The Stock Market and Social Security Reform," August 9, 2002. Available at http://www.cato.org/dailys/08-09-02.html.

153 *Generational lottery*   Christine E. Weller, "Social Security Privatization: The Retirement Savings Gamble," Center for American Progress, February 2005.

153 *Political pressure*   Diamond and Orszag, p. 147.

155 *Few can control*   Munnell et al., "Yikes! How to Think About Risk," Boston University Center for Retirement Research, Issue Brief 27, January 2005.

158 *quite loose, and quite mysterious*   Tobin, p. 4.

160 *Our general presumption* Friedman, in Michael D. Tanner (ed.), *Social Security and Its Discontents,* p. 312.

161 *Many workers* Tobin, p. 19.

162 *EBRI study* EBRI Issue Brief 272, August 2004. See also an analysis in "Money Trouble—A Lesson for Social Security," *Wall Street Journal,* December 1, 2004.

163 *Performance of self-managed 401(k) plans* Alicia H. Munnell, *Coming Up Short,* Brookings Institution, 2004.

163 *It's not at all clear* Personal communication.

163 *In real life* Thomas Geoghegan, "The Hassle Factor of Retiring Solvent," *Chicago Tribune,* March 9, 2005.

164 *The average large plan* Munnell.

164 *If that were to happen, the same people* Schieber and Shoven, p. 363.

168 *Indeed, few proposals* Diamond and Orszag, p. 145.

168 *They would undermine* Ibid.

Chapter 10: The Ownership Scam 2

169 *Impossible* Statement of Francis X. Cavanaugh, Subcommittee on Social Security, June 18, 1998.

170 *Administrative costs would eat deeply* "Administrative Costs of Private Accounts in Social Security," Congressional Budget Office, March 2004, Table 1-1, p. 2.

170 *mating a bear with a bee* Francis X. Cavanaugh, "Feasibility of Social Security Individual Accounts," Public Policy Institute, AARP, 2002.

172 *No existing system* John M. Kimpel, "Administrative Constraints on Individual Social Security Accounts," in Dallas Salisbury (ed.), *Beyond Ideology: Are Individual Social Security Accounts Feasible?* Employee Benefit Research Institute, 1999.

173 *We don't see them* President's Commission to Strengthen Social Security, August 22, 2001, session transcript, p. 32.

175 *outside the scope* Cavanaugh.

176 *Fidelity performed 450 million* Kimpel, p. 167.

177 *as many as 100,000* Ibid., p. 166.

180 *really a down payment* Feldstein, Keynote Address, *Social Security: The Opportunity for Real Reform,* Cato Institute, February 8, 2005.

182 *Fully half the pension contributions* "Keeping the Promise of Old Age Income Security in Latin America," at www.worldbank.org /lacpensionsconf, p. 8.

182 *Although the government reformed*   R. Fischer, P. Gonzales, and P. Serra, "The Privatization of Social Services in Chile: An Evaluation," Centro de Economia Aplicada, Document No. 167, p. 5.

183 *The fund managers*   Ibid., p. 7.

Chapter 11: Bush Stacks the Deck

186 *O'Neill and president-elect*   Ron Suskind, *The Price of Loyalty,* p. 28.

186 *convinced . . . that it was appropriate*   Ibid., p. 49.

187 *As O'Neill recalled thinking*   Ibid., p. 39.

187 *At one Oval Office meeting*   Ibid., pp. 152–53.

188 *Nothing exemplified this*   Ibid., p. 156.

190 *In convening the first official meeting*   Transcript of June 11, 2001, meeting, at http://www.csss.gov/meetings/transcripts/June_11_transcript.pdf, p.61.

191 *did not dictate*   Andrew Biggs, in Tanner, p. 204.

191 *Mitchell . . . had published*   See John Geanakoplos, Olivia S. Mitchell, and Steven Zeldes, "Would a Privatized Social Security System Really Pay a Higher Rate of Return?" in Arnold, Graetz, and Munnell (eds.), *Framing the Social Security Debate,* p. 137 ff.

193 *When Commissioner Robert Johnson*   June 11, 2001, transcript, pp. 89–90.

197 *Moynihan has expressed*   Memorandum, Kent Smetters to O'Neill, October 15, 2001, available at http://thepriceofloyalty.ronsuskind.com/thebushfiles/archives/000097.html.

197 *A week later*   Smetters to O'Neill, October 22, 2001, available at http://thepriceofloyalty.ronsuskind.com/thebushfiles/archives/000099.html.

197 *Moynihan became particularly irked*   Smetters to O'Neill, November 20, 2001, available at http://thepriceofloyalty.ronsuskind.com/thebushfiles/archives/000098.html.

201 *share in the general increase*   Peter Diamond and Peter R. Orszag, "An Assessment of the Proposals of the President's Commission to Strengthen Social Security," *Contributions to Economic Analysis and Policy,* vol. 1, no. 1, 2002.

202 *As economist Edward Gramlich . . . noted*   Wall Street Journal Online, December 19, 2004, quoted in Orszag, testimony before House Committee on the Budget, February 9, 2005.

202 *The number of elderly*   Economic Policy Institute *Snapshot,* February 9, 2005.

203 *$4.7 trillion in transition costs*   Diamond and Orszag, op. cit., p. 41.

203 *Not "a single mention"*   Ibid., p. 29.

Chapter 12: Operation Shock and Awe

205 *The 44-year-old Wehner*   Dan Balz, "Resident Thinker Given Free Rein in White House," *Washington Post,* December 13, 2004.

207 *I already do an awful lot of speeches*   Don Jordan, "A&M Professor to Advise Social Security Reformers," *Houston Chronicle,* February 24, 2005.

208 *Agency employees presently complained*   "The Politicization of the Social Security Administration," Committee on Government Reform, Minority Staff, House of Representatives, February 2005, p. 1.

208 *growing politicization*   Ibid., p. ii.

208 *massive and growing shortfall*   Ibid.

208 *most basic public primer*   Ibid., p. 5.

Chapter 13: What's Really Wrong with Social Security

224 *When these factors*   "Internal Real Rates of Return Under the OASDI Program for Hypothetical Workers," Actuarial Note No. 144, June 2001, Social Security Administration, at www.ssa.gov/OACT/NOTES/note2000s/note144.html.

225 *The longevity statistics do hint*   See Diamond and Orszag, p. 68.

225 *the trend reduces*   Ibid., p. 69.

232 *A different approach*   Diamond and Orszag, p. 82.

234 *It therefore seems appropriate*   Ibid., p. 90.

235 *As Diamond and Orszag point out*   Ibid., p. 215.

235 *One social group*   See Aaron, discussant, in Arnold, Graetz, and Munnell (eds.), p. 179.

237 *The government spent $85 billion*   "Private Pensions: Issues of Coverage and Increasing Contribution Limits for Defined Contribution Plans," General Accounting Office, September 2001.

240 *If the tax cuts*   Estimates of the value of the Social Security deficit over the 75-year and infinite horizons are from the 2004 report of the Social Security trustees, p. 59. Estimates of the cost of the tax cuts are from Richard Kogan and Robert Greenstein, "President Portrays Social Security Shortfall as Enormous," Center on Budget and Policy Priorities, February 2, 2005.

240 *One good candidate for such a role*   Diamond and Orszag, p. 94.

Bibliography

Aaron, Henry J., and Robert D. Reischauer, *Countdown to Reform: The Great Social Security Debate*. New York: Century Foundation, 2001.

Arnold, R. Douglas, Michael J. Graetz, and Alicia H. Munnell (eds.): *Framing the Social Security Debate: Values, Politics, and Economics*. Washington, D.C.: National Academy of Social Insurance, 1998.

Baker, Dean, and Mark Weisbrot: *Social Security: The Phony Crisis*. Chicago: University of Chicago Press, 1999.

Ball, Robert M.: *Insuring the Essentials: Bob Ball on Social Security*. New York: Century Foundation, 2000.

Berkowitz, Edward D.: *Robert Ball and the Politics of Social Security*. Madison, Wisc.: University of Wisconsin Press, 2003.

Boskin, Michael J.: *Too Many Promises: The Uncertain Future of Social Security*. Homewood, Ill.: Dow Jones-Irwin, 1986.

Cannon, Lou: *President Reagan: The Role of a Lifetime*. New York: PublicAffairs, 2000.

Clinton, Bill: *My Life*. New York: Alfred A. Knopf, 2004.

Davis, Kenneth S.: *FDR, The New Deal Years, 1933–1937*. New York: Random House, 1979.

Diamond, Peter A., and Peter R. Orszag, *Saving Social Security: A Balanced Approach*. Washington, D.C.: Brookings Institution Press, 2004.

Feldstein, Martin (ed.): *Privatizing Social Security*. Chicago: University of Chicago Press, 1998.

Friedman, Milton, and Rose D. Friedman, *Free to Choose*. New York: Harcourt, 1980.

BIBLIOGRAPHY

Glassman, James K., and Kevin A. Hassett: *Dow 36,000*. New York: Crown Business, 1999.

Hardy, Dorcas, and C. Colburn Hardy: *Social Insecurity: The Crisis in America's Social Security System and How to Plan Now for Your Own Financial Survival*. New York: Villard Books, 1991.

Johnson, David Cay: *Perfectly Legal*. New York: Portfolio, 2003.

Kotlikoff, Lawrence J., and Scott Burns: *The Coming Generational Storm*. Cambridge, Mass.: MIT Press, 2004.

Leuchtenburg, William E.: *Franklin D. Roosevelt and the New Deal*. New York: Harper & Row, 1963.

Munnell, Alicia H.: *The Future of Social Security*. Washington, D.C.: Brookings Institution, 1977.

Peterson, Peter G.: *Running on Empty*. New York: Farrar, Straus and Giroux, 2004.

Reagan, Ronald: *An American Life*. New York: Simon & Schuster, 1990.

Schieber, Sylvester J., and John R. Shoven: *The Real Deal: The History and Future of Social Security*. New Haven: Yale University Press, 1999.

Schlesinger, Arthur M. Jr.: *The Age of Roosevelt: The Politics of Upheaval*. Boston: Houghton Mifflin, 1960.

Smith, Allen W.: *The Looting of Social Security*. New York: Carroll & Graf, 2004.

Stockman, David A.: *The Triumph of Politics*. New York: Harper & Row, 1986.

Suskind, Ron: *The Price of Loyalty: George W. Bush, the White House, and the Education of Paul O'Neill*. New York: Simon & Schuster, 2004.

Tanner, Michael D. (ed.): *Social Security and Its Discontents: Perspectives on Choice*. Washington, D.C.: Cato Institute, 2004.

White, Joseph: *False Alarm: Why the Greatest Threat to Social Security and Medicare Is the Campaign to "Save" Them*. Baltimore: Johns Hopkins University Press, 2001.